Heaven in Ordinary

Heaven in Ordinary

A Poet's Corner Collection

Malcolm Guite

CANTERBURY
PRESS
Norwich

First published in 2020 by the Canterbury Press Norwich
Editorial office
3rd Floor, Invicta House
108–114 Golden Lane
London EC1Y 0TG, UK
www.canterburypress.co.uk

Canterbury Press is an imprint of Hymns Ancient & Modern Ltd
(a registered charity)

Hymns Ancient & Modern® is a registered trademark of Hymns
Ancient & Modern Ltd
13A Hellesdon Park Road, Norwich,
Norfolk NR6 5DR, UK

British Library Cataloguing in Publication data

A catalogue record for this book is available
from the British Library

978 1-78622-262-6

Typeset by Regent Typesetting

Contents

Preface

It is has been a pleasure to gather together these short essays, written week by week, reflecting on the little incidents of life, the occasional hints and glints of insight that shimmer into being with a change in the light or a shift in one's own perspective. Most of these essays touch on places and experiences in the common run of things rather than the far-fetched or exotic: the sound of church bells, a journey through the villages of Suffolk, a parish outing to Great Yarmouth. They touch on the pleasure of turning the pages of a familiar book, watching the motes of dust dance in a sudden shaft of sunlight, pausing for a moment to watch the progress of a village cricket match – the ordinary things, often unremarked on in an unremarkable life. And yet my experience in writing, in pausing to give these things attention, in seeking to sound them out into language and catch a little of their transience in a net of words, has brought me back time and again to George Herbert's telling phrase 'Heaven in Ordinary'. As I reflected in the little essay that gives this book its title: 'All of us who have read Herbert's poem and savoured this phrase can have an immediate sense of what he means: that prayer itself sometimes lifts a veil and allows us to see the ordinary and everyday transfigured for a moment – to glimpse the temporal made suddenly lucid and lucent with a touch of eternity.'

The phrase always seems to summon that other famous verse of Herbert's that we sing together in church:

A man that looks on glass,
On it may stay his eye;

Or if he pleaseth, through it pass,
And then the heaven espy.

Just for a moment, the glassy surface of the world, dusty and familiar, is cleared and cleansed; something shines through, and we have a brief anticipation of St Paul's great hope for us all: that although 'now we see through a glass darkly', one day 'we shall know as we are known'; one day 'we shall see face to face', and the face we shall see is the face of Love'.

So I have two hopes for this little book. The first, of course, is that you will enjoy my own small glimpses of 'Heaven in ordinary'; that you will savour with me some simple pleasures, and delight with me in seeing how much survives of the past – in turns of phrase, in the lie of the land, in the streets of our villages and the pews of our churches, and on the shelves in our studies – to nurture the present; that you will have pleasure, and even gain some insight, in gazing with me at the ripples on a pond, enjoying the fall of snow or supping a pint in an old pub. But second, I do hope that when you put down the book you will be encouraged to go out yourself with a more leisurely step, a more observant eye and an inclination to notice and savour those little glimpses of 'Heaven in ordinary' that open to us everywhere.

Finally, I should remark that almost all these pieces were written before the coronavirus crisis came upon us, and indeed I could have filled the whole book with pieces written, in that sense, 'BC', but I have chosen to end the book with two pieces that touch on the new reality. 'A Message from Wuhan' tells of how I heard from someone isolated there, before our own isolation had even been imagined, who had found her faith strengthened and deepened by the example of Julian of Norwich – an expert on self-isolation if ever there was one. It was good to know that however 'novel' this virus may be we have been here before and our faith has the resources to help us cope. And the final piece of this book comes from that first Easter in lockdown, and takes from John Donne's 'Death Be Not Proud' a note of courage and defiance. Like Julian of Norwich, John Donne saw more than his fair share of 'poison, war, and sickness', but he could still fling this great defiance into the face of death. As we move into a new phase of our history, and of our Christian witness, I wanted to end my book on that note of defiance, for 'It is Christ's defiance, and it is ours'.

1

A Handful of Dust

Set among the pen trays, inkstands, paperweights and general clutter on my desk is a little box full of fine red dirt – so fine as to be almost dust. I brought it home with me from a remarkable place: the Santuario de Chimayó, in a hidden valley high in the Sangre de Cristo Mountains of New Mexico.

I made a pilgrimage there with the American poet Scott Cairns. As we came close to the shrine, all along the ledges and fences at the side of the path, pilgrims before us had tied rosaries, left messages and photographs, and leaned the wooden crosses that some of them had carried on their journey.

The story of this strange place, amid mountains called after the blood of Christ, is as much bound up with the cross as it is with the red dirt of the high desert. The site had long been sacred to the Tewa, a tribe of Pueblo Native Americans, and when they became Christians, this remarkable place remained a sacred site.

For the story goes that, one night, a poor farmer saw a light in the hills, and when he came to investigate he found, shining through the red dust, a large crucifix. Thinking it must belong to the Spanish monks in Santa Cruz, he put it in his donkey cart and brought it to them, and they placed it on their altar; but when he returned to his place in the hills, there it was again, in the hole where he had found it.

This happened three times, and the third time the monks agreed that it was a sign that Christ was just as much with the native people in the pueblo as he was with the settlers in Santa Cruz; so they built a church there, and very soon it became a healing shrine.

But the fascinating thing is that although the miraculous crucifix is still there, on the altar of that mountain church, it is not the altar, but just behind it, the 'El Pocito', the shallow hole in the red dirt where the cross was found, that is the sacred place. People come to hear mass in the church but, in the end, they kneel on the dusty earth and lift a little dirt from the ground with their hands, as I did, to pray for healing and wholeness.

I don't know what to make of the legends, but I had no doubt that I was in a holy place, and that the crutches and walking frames left behind were testimony to changed lives. I also felt there a strong integration and continuity between the new faith and the old: a sense that Christ had confirmed and brought to perfection what God had already and always been doing in that place.

I thought, too, as I knelt and touched the dirt, of how Adam, the name Genesis gives to all humanity, means red clay; of how good it is to know that we come from the dust of our mother earth. I thought of how, in dying, the second Adam was content to go down into that dust with us; of how, as John Donne says, 'that blood which is The seat of all our Soules, if not of his' was 'Made dirt of dust', and how, on Easter Day, that dust was raised again to begin our new humanity.

So as I look on it now, the little box of dust on my desk is not so much a *memento mori* as a *memento vitae*.

2

A Falling Leaf

This morning, I took a Sunday walk with George and Zara, the two retired greyhounds whose job it is to teach me returning and rest.

We ambled through bright autumn sunlight, beneath some trees on the fringes of the village green, and I paused to watch a single leaf fall, effortlessly, and find its place, exactly in the centre of a tessellated pattern of red and gold, as though placed and fitted there by the last touch of an intent and careful artist.

Indeed, the leaf did not so much fall as descend gently in a fine, flattening curve, and in its last movement glide almost horizontally, inches above the ground, before settling, stilled, quieted, perfect. The air seemed still to me, and yet that smooth flight told me that the leaf was winging on some imperceptibly small current; that the perfect curve of its gentle descent expressed, outwardly and visibly, a balance between those two invisible mysteries that shape our world: gravity and air.

These moments of beauty are everywhere, almost always unobserved – a part of the 'charge' of the 'grandeur of God', as Hopkins called it, that fills and fulfils the world with something overflowing: a pleroma, an uncountable abundance that we mostly miss.

Thankful that I hadn't missed this moment, I recalled the opening words of one of Wendell Berry's 'Sabbaths' poems in which he speaks of resuming 'the long lesson' of learning again how a small thing can be pleasing if we will only pay attention.

In his great essay 'The Redress of Poetry', Seamus Heaney says that poetry 'offers a clarification, a fleeting glimpse of a potential order of things "beyond confusion", a glimpse that has to be its own reward'.

I once had a conversation with him in which he developed that idea further. 'Sometimes,' he said, 'it is not necessarily the whole poem, or the poem as it is read on the page, but just a phrase or two that comes to you, surfaces in your mind in the right place at the right time and offers you phrases that feed the soul.'

I felt that Berry was offering me just that. Wandering beneath the trees with my dogs, more phrases from his 'Sabbaths' poem came to my mind, phrases that had the effect of focusing and clarifying for me where I was and what I was seeing, poised between time and eternity. Berry speaks of how the trees rise in silence and how that natural silence is 'almost eternal, but not quite'.

The end of that poem does something even more remarkable; for the poet sees that the person on his sabbath walk, whose mind rests in the sight of the falling leaf, delighting in its goodness and beauty, is himself participating in a deeper rest and a greater beholding, in which the 'Maker of all this' beholds all things, both man and leaf. For a moment he feels the mind of God, in its eternal sabbath, resting in his own mind and offering him, in that moment, the chance to participate in that rest, as he and God watch 'a yellow leaf slowly / falling' and take pleasure in it together.

3

Ordinary Saints

I returned recently from a weekend retreat, which included the first 'performance' (though that's not quite the right word) of 'Ordinary Saints', an event combining image, poetry and music, including the sequence of 'ekphrastic' poems that I composed in response to a set of portraits by the American artist Bruce Herman, about which I wrote briefly in an earlier Poet's Corner in the *Church Times*.

It was a remarkable experience. We gathered in a gallery with all 26 portraits, and heard the poems and music – sometimes separately, sometimes combined – that the portraits had inspired. These were not portraits of the rich or famous, or necessarily of people who had achieved great things. They were paintings of 'ordinary people': the artist's family and friends, but all created with loving attention, meticulous detail and, most of all, an eye for the inner person; for the singing soul, shining through the skin; for the image of God, shimmering for a moment through the dark glass of our seeing; hinting, the artist hoped, at transfiguration.

My title poem for the sequence, introducing the themes all three of us – poet, painter and composer – wanted to explore, asked the questions:

> … Who can truly show
> Whilst still rough-hewn, the God who shapes our ends?
> Who will unveil the presence, glimpse the gold
> That is and always was our common ground,
> Stretch out a finger, feel, along the fold,
> To find the flaw, to touch and search that wound
> From which the light we never noticed fell
> Into our lives?

The aim was not simply to focus on these particular paintings or the people who had sat for them, rather it was to enable those who had spent time with the portraits to see one another in a new way.

In one sense, we were seeking, in Herbert's great phrase, to see 'Heaven in ordinary'; but, in another, we were responding to an insight of C. S. Lewis's, in his celebrated sermon 'The Weight of Glory': 'There are no ordinary people. You have never talked to a mere mortal ... Next to the Blessed Sacrament itself, your neighbour is the holiest object presented to your senses. If he is your Christian neighbour, he is holy in almost the same way; for in him also Christ *vere latitat* [truly hides], the glorifier and the glorified, Glory Himself, is truly hidden.'

So after we had seen the portraits, and seen them again in the light of the poetry and music, we finished the retreat with a Eucharist; and just before we exchanged the peace, we turned and faced one another as I read the final poem in the sequence:

And now we turn our eyes from wood and paint
To contemplate the saints in flesh and blood,
The ones who've seen these pictures with us. Faint
Traces of God's image, and his glad
Presence in humanity, have shone
Awhile for us in paintings on a wall,
The dark glass brightened, and the shadows gone.
How shall we know each other now? Will all
That we have seen recede to memory?
Or is our sight restored, and having gazed
On icons in this place, will clarity
Transfigure all of us? We turn, amazed,
To see the ones beside us, face to face,
As living icons, sacraments of grace.

4

Crisis and Some Other Words

Is it wrong, I thought, as I leaned on the railing of the Lady Bridge in Linton, and watched the Granta's clear stream go curling and rippling beneath me, bearing the last of autumn's flame-coloured leaves away to their rest – is it wrong to contemplate and rest in these ephemeral beauties, while the country is in crisis?

Or does the contemplation of our village stream, at once an emblem of all that passes, and of all that remains, comfort and clarify the mind, so that it can bear to turn once more to the speculations, the rumours and the forebodings that accompany political crisis?

Actually, it was the word 'crisis' that occupied my thoughts as George and Zara tugged at their leads and nudged me into continuing our morning walk. The present crisis turns, I thought, on issues of national identity; but, ironically, the word for which we all reach is not English, but Greek. Rooted in the Greek verb *krinein*, 'to decide', it was taken over in Latin to mean a decision and, by extension, a decisive turning-point; and then came into Late Middle English via medical Latin, where it meant the decisive turning-point, for better or worse, of a disease.

All of its many senses seem apposite now. The word 'crisis' also summoned up, for me, memories of doing 'the Tragedy Paper' as an undergraduate. We wrote essays on Greek tragedy before we were allowed to tackle Shakespeare, and crisis was one of a clutch of three Greek words with which we had to be familiar; the other two, coming to my mind unbidden as I crossed the Granta again on my walk, also seemed strangely and strongly relevant: hubris and catharsis.

There has been plenty of scope in our national life for

noticing hubris: the overweening pride that precedes comeuppance and calamity, although people might differ over which of the current players are most hubristic. But beyond the crisis brought on by hubris there is the possibility of catharsis, purification, cleansing: the experience, even vicariously, of pity and fear, felt so deeply that they might lead to renewal and clarity, might deliver us from hubris and undo its damage.

So I continued on my morning walk, revolving my three Greek words, wandering past St Mary's, the little church that had seen its village through many a crisis, weathered civil war, reformation and revolution, absorbed and expressed in its patient grey stone the hopes, fears and prayers of 800 years of local living.

I took some comfort in that, and the sight of the church made me reach for a fourth Greek word, a word we were never taught in the Tragedy Paper but which I learned when I came back to Cambridge, years later, to train as a priest, a word Christ himself can bring to all our tragedy: *agape*. When Homer used that word, it simply meant affection, but on the lips of Christ and in the writings of Paul, it was trans-figured into something far deeper: the love that bears all things, believes all things, hopes all things, that never fails.

When we come through this crisis, whatever lies on the far side of it, we are going to need – to receive and to share – all the *agape* we can get. Thank God that, in Christ, there is a limitless supply.

5

A Muddy Field

Last Saturday, I joined other villagers in a muddy field on the edge of Linton for what proved to be a revelation. The same field whose unremarkable acres we had all ambled past and ignored was laid open now, a good depth of its topsoil dug away and piled in mounds round its perimeter, to reveal a variegated substrate of flinty chalk, darker patterns of older, deeper earth showing against the white, and then, exposed in various places, the first pits and hollows of an archaeological dig.

The field was earmarked for a new housing development, but first there was to be some thorough archaeology, and when the archaeologists offered the village a guided tour, it turned out we were all just as curious about our ancient neighbours as we will be about the new ones when they eventually move in.

I was fascinated by the way even comparatively shallow excavations could yield and reveal so much. A path of dark clay and stone, running over the white chalk, was the old road, buried all this time, which yielded eighteenth-century carriage bolts that had been shaken loose over its rough surface; and then, off to one side, deeper and beautifully curved and lined down into the chalk, a medieval well, twelfth or thirteenth century, that served more medieval dwellings in the field above.

But as we followed the slope of the field down into the shallow valley of the Granta, we came to older things: the post-holes and footings of early Anglo-Saxon sunken houses, from which the archaeologists had taken, from the place it had been discarded, a beautifully made little comb.

Then, further down, on what would have been the edge of a once much broader river, they had found, and were able to show us, hundreds of worked flint shards and offcuttings – the 'spoil' of systematic flint-working from the Mesolithic period – and so we knew that the flint that we held in our hands had been worked and handled by someone walking over this ground more than 10,000 years ago.

We stood in the wind and rain, amazed. That sense of sheer continuity is strengthening in one way, but dizzying in another. I remembered Larkin's observation in 'Reference Back' that, even though our element is time, 'We are not suited to the long perspectives.'

Only last week, I was taking comfort, in the midst of national crisis, in the thought that our parish church had served its village continuously for '800 years of local living'; but what is that to the tens of thousands of years opening up just a few feet beneath our boots in an ordinary field? Not long after, I would hear on the radio about the successful landing on Mars, and how the human spirit, extended by an ingenious machine, was setting about the same gentle digging, the same meticulous inquiry and recording that motivated the archaeologists here.

And I knew that the span from the flint tool in my hand to the InSight lander on Mars is only an inch on the long line of our prehistory. What measure can contain the past that opens under us, and the future we cannot see?

I was glad, on Sunday, to be reminded that our little interval, however brief, is part of a coherent whole; and glad to hear and ponder those words 'I am the Alpha and the Omega.'

6

The Winter Moon

As nights grow darker and longer I see more of the moon, and am drawn, like every poet, to her mystery, her pallor, her luminous and beautiful changes. Were I more of an astronomer, or if I remembered more of those early episodes of *The Sky At Night*, I suppose I would know where to look for her, in what quarter she would be resplendent, and at which hour, and none of her phases would surprise me.

As it is, my ignorance allows me a series of happy surprises: the veil of a cloud is drawn aside and there she is again, unexpectedly new, unfathomably old. And the pleasure of gazing on the moon is, of course, intensified by memory – not just the memory of other moonlit nights but of all the poets who have gazed on her before, from lovelorn Philip Sidney, imagining the moon as wan and sad as himself –

With how sad steps, O Moon, thou climb'st the skies!
How silently, and with how wan a face!

– to a rueful Philip Larkin, answering Sidney, in the poem 'Sad Steps', and startled by the 'Far-reaching singleness of that wide stare'.

As I gaze on the moon tonight, I am neither lovelorn, sad, nor rueful, just poignantly aware of how her reflected light gathers so many memories and reflects them back as both change and constancy. Even as I glimpse her through my study window while I am writing this, I have a sudden and vivid memory of staring at the moon through another window, on another winter's night.

It was a high window, in a high room: a hospital ward

11

in Cambridge, where I lay, fasted and empty, waiting for an operation to mend a broken leg, an operation that kept being postponed kept me on 'Nil by mouth', my only companion a comforting, if strangely dislocating, drip of morphine. My tired mind was just slipping into a Coleridgean free-wheeling reverie when clouds parted and the full moon herself slipped into view.

In her light, the falling snow made strange and beautiful patterns that seemed to lift me, assisted perhaps by the morphine, up towards the moon herself. I tried to capture it in these lines:

The moon is full and snow falls soft tonight
In silver filigree. I seem to fall,
Floating through the chapel of her light,
The moon is full.

The white lace of the snowfall makes a veil
Through which I glimpse her face, a paler white,
Whose pallor calls to me, a tidal pull

That gathers in me, loosens, lifts the weight
That palls and pulls me. In her light I feel
Fasted and lifted, empty, open, light,
The moon is full.

That was years ago, and now, just as in Keats's 'The Eve of St Agnes', 'full on the casement' shines 'the wintry moon'. Unfortunately for her, she does not shine on the beautiful Madeline saying her prayers, 'her hands together pressed … and on her hair a glory like a saint'; she shines, instead, on a grey-haired man in his cluttered study; but he too makes a chapel of the moonlight, and he too is about to say his prayers.

7

Swaddling Bands

'Ye shall find the babe wrapped in swaddling clothes, lying in a manger.'

There is something strangely attractive about the word 'swaddling'. It comes, through Middle English, from 'swathe', which meant both a path and a strip of material, and then came to mean the act of wrapping up closely. So Wycliffe's translation of Luke had Jesus wrapped in 'swathing clothes'.

The word 'swaddling' carries with it a sense of closeness and comfort, and yet also suggests that there will be freedom and release in the unwrapping.

Lancelot Andrewes, the great preacher and contributing translator of the Authorized Version, also reflected on this word. In his famous Christmas sermon on Christ as the *Verbum infans*, 'the Word without a word', a sermon that had such a strong influence on T. S. Eliot, Andrewes says of the word 'swaddled':

> and that a wonder too. 'He, that (as the thirty-eighth of Job he saith) taketh the vast body of the main sea, turns it to and fro, as a little child, and rolls it about with the swaddling bands of darkness;' – He to come thus into clouts, Himself!

It's a wonderful image from Job, of the sea turned to and fro in the swaddling bands of darkness. And then Andrewes brings it all home to the stable again with that common word 'clouts', still preserved for us in the saying 'Ne're cast a clout till May be out'.

Luther too was drawn to the image of Christ wrapped in swaddling bands. In his introduction to the Old Testament he described the pages of the Bible as being like the swaddling clothes in which Mary wrapped Jesus:

> Here (in the Scripture) you will find the swaddling-clothes and the manger in which Christ lies, and to which the angel points the shepherds. Simple and little are the swaddling-clothes, but dear is the treasure, Christ, that lies in them.

John Donne took Luther up on that, and in a sermon on the use and abuse of Scripture said that we must turn each page of the Bible as though we were turning back the cloth that wraps our Saviour: our sole purpose is to reveal the radiance of the living Christ. If we use the words of Scripture for any purpose other than to show Christ and his love, they no longer have authority or contain treasure but are just rags.

That image of the precious and eternal, wrapped for a while in rags, seems to have spoken deeply to Donne, and he came to see that it is true of each of us too: that the eternity in each of us is wrapped for a while in time; but that sometimes, at moments of great spiritual or emotional intensity, time itself seems to fall away from us in rags. So in an exaltation of love, in his poem 'The Sunne Rising', he says:

> Love, all alike, no season knows, nor clime,
> Nor hours, days, months, which are the rags of time.

And he returns to that great phrase from the love poetry of his youth, when, as Dean of St Paul's, he wanted to speak of God's mercy:

> We begin with that which is elder than our beginning, and shall overlive our end, the mercy of God … The names of first and last derogate from it, for first and last are but rags

14

of time, and his mercy hath no relation to time, no limitation in time, it is not first nor last, but eternal, everlasting.

For me, the promise that one day the rags of time will fall away from us is at once the promise of new birth and the promise of resurrection, and I have always felt some sense of connection between the swaddling cloths of which the angels spoke at Christmas and the linen cloths that Jesus left lying folded in his empty tomb where the angels stood.

I wove together all these feelings and presentiments, as though they too were swaddling bands, when I came to write 'O Emmanuel', the final poem in my sequence on the Advent Antiphons.

For Advent led me to look forward not only to Christmas but also beyond Christmas, to a new birth for humanity and for the whole cosmos, which is promised through the birth of God in our midst. Because the birth of Christ is itself the sign of the other birth that Christ promises: the birth of the Kingdom of God, and ourselves born anew within it.

O come, O come, and be our God-with-us,
O long-sought with-ness for a world without,
O secret seed, O hidden spring of light.
Come to us Wisdom, come unspoken Name,
Come Root, and Key, and King, and holy Flame.
O quickened little wick so tightly curled,
Be folded with us into time and place,
Unfold for us the mystery of grace
And make a womb of all this wounded world.
O heart of heaven beating in the earth,
O tiny hope within our hopelessness,
Come to be born, to bear us to our birth,
To touch a dying world with new-made hands
And make these rags of time our swaddling bands.

8

Church Bells

One of the pleasures of this season in Linton is in hearing the bells rung from St Mary's church tower: the sound of bells called us to the Christmas services, and bells ring in the New Year. Indeed, many parishioners keep New Year's Eve with the ringers, in a bring-and-share feast in our church pavilion, and then toast the New Year with them when they come down from ringing it in.

I am no campanologist and, like many people, my knowledge of the distinctively English art of change-ringing is entirely beholden to close readings and re-readings of Dorothy Sayers' masterpiece *The Nine Tailors*.

But I know enough, as the bells summon me to church, to listen for their intricate interweaving, each with its own tone and name, changing places in a complex dance, answering one another. I hear it as a kind of metre, a kind of poetry, and it is no surprise that this art in ringing has inspired the art of many poets.

George Herbert, in his beautiful poem 'Prayer I' – which is itself a kind of peal, a ringing out of 27 images in 14 lines, each image an emblem of prayer – makes one of those emblems the sound of bells: 'Church-bells beyond the stars heard.' There is a fine ambiguity there, for Herbert leaves us to decide whether it is heaven that hears our bells or we who sometimes, in our prayer, hear the bells from beyond the stars, the music of the spheres.

Milton invokes those same spheres in the famous lines of his 'On the Morning of Christ's Nativity':

Ring out, ye crystal spheres!
Once bless our human ears,
(If ye have power to touch our senses so)

Nearly 150 years later, it was the sound of church bells, heard in childhood, that first stirred and haunted Coleridge with those longings that eventually found their fulfilment in Christ.

> … the old church-tower,
> Whose bells, the poor man's only music, rang
> From morn to evening, all the hot Fair-day,
> So sweetly, that they stirred and haunted me
> With a wild pleasure, falling on mine ear
> Most like articulate sounds of things to come!

Tennyson, who surely knew and loved this passage, takes up the peal and rings his own changes on it, in the great outburst of joy and hope that pierces the long darkness of his *In Memoriam*:

> Ring out, wild bells, to the wild sky,
> The flying cloud, the frosty light:
> The year is dying in the night;
> Ring out, wild bells, and let him die.

Betjeman too was famously 'summoned by bells', and I also tried once, in my own small way, to answer the summons of those bells, in my poem 'New Year's Day: Church Bells', which began by contrasting the long, strong continuity of those old bells with the more recent noises of our electronica:

> Not the bleak speak of mobile messages,
> The soft chime of synthesized reminders,

17

Not texts, not pagers, data packages,
Not satnav or locators ever find us
As surely, soundly, deeply as these bells …

And I ended my poem with an attempt to render in the
sound of the lines themselves something of the music our
change-ringers set flying through the frosty air:

'Begin again' they sing, 'again begin',
A ring and rhythm answered from within.

9

Peace

We are in Aldeburgh again, seeking a little post-Christmas peace and quiet in our favourite seaside town, and already the steady rhythms of wave and tide, the drift of aromatic woodsmoke from the sheds where they cure the daily catch, and the whole old-fashioned charm of the place have begun to work their magic and relax us.

Of course, there is an irony in seeking 'post-Christmas peace', if one were to understand the word 'peace' in any of its deeper senses. For however hectic, bustled and occasionally stressful the ceremonies and hospitalities of Christmas may have been, a proclamation of peace is at their heart: peace and good will from heaven to earth, and so also among ourselves. And that Christmas peace is no mere glib greeting but real peace, real reconciliation between earth and heaven, between our conscience and our Creator, bought with the heart's blood of the Prince of Peace and offered to us where we are and as we are.

In fact that deeper peace, that peace that is entirely given, but not as the world gives, has been on my heart and mind because, on this holiday, I am working on a new sequence of meditative poems responding to George Herbert's beautiful, riddling poem 'Prayer I', in which, over a mere 14 lines, he offers 27 images or emblems of prayer, and one of them is simply the word 'peace'.

Knowing how often Herbert was downcast and how much he struggled with himself and with the world, I knew that he could not mean some easy shallow peace, some mere well-wishing. Struggling with my poetic response, I was also aware, as we put Christmas behind us, of how swiftly all the seasonal wishes of peace and good will from our politicians seem to have evaporated.

After a blessed break from all the Brexit furore, at least in the media, I fear that by the time you read this, January will have returned us to the fray, with redoubled demonizing, extra denigration and a continuing impasse, begetting nothing but impotent fury from all sides. There are vital things at stake, of course, and there is a proper passion about them; but wandering past Aldeburgh's Tudor Moot Hall, the scene, over centuries, of no doubt vigorous local debate, I prayed also for the Houses of Parliament, that there might be as much charity as passion in the moot points debated there.

But as I composed my poem on peace as prayer and prayer as peace, I found myself also looking inwards at everything in me that has not made for peace, and longing for peace not as another task, another goal we signally fail to achieve, but as sheer gift, release and relief, something to be received just as thankfully alongside our opponents as among our friends.

So the poem came out like this:

Peace

Not as the world gives, not the victor's peace,
Not to be fought for, hard-won, or achieved,
Just grace and mercy, gratefully received:
An undeserved and unforeseen release,
As the cold chains of memory and wrath
Fall from our hearts before we are aware,
Their rusty locks all picked by patient prayer,
Till closed doors open, and we see a path
Descending from a source we cannot see;

A path that must be taken, hand in hand,
Only by those, forgiving and forgiven,
Who see their saviour in their enemy.
So reach for me, we'll cross our broken land,
And make each other bridges back to Heaven.

10

Re-Entry

I remember reading an interview once with an astronaut who had just returned from a spell in the International Space Station. 'What was re-entry like?' he was asked. 'What did it feel like to fall to earth again and return home?'

Perhaps the interviewer was hoping for an encomium on the joys of homecoming: how precious the earth was, how sweet the rain smelt, how good it was to be back. But what the astronaut said was that, on his return to earth, the first thing he felt was the oppression of unaccustomed weight. He felt overweight, sluggish, hardly able to lift a hand, and there was a stale and smoky tang in the air from the burn-up on re-entry.

And that is exactly how many of us feel on returning to work in January: coming down, suddenly heavier, after our free-floating holidays.

And for those of us who resume the privilege and burden of pastoral care, there is an even deeper, perhaps heavier sense of returning gravity; for we often come back to the *gravitas* of sorrow. We come back to organize and conduct January funerals, to pick up, to knit up again, the ravelled threads of parish tragedies, and it takes us a while to adjust.

But perhaps the parallel experience of that astronaut has something to offer here as well; for in that interview I recall him saying that, after the first dismay of unaccustomed weight, he did bring back to daily life a new perspective: the astonishing sight of the earth from afar, an epiphany in all its blue-green beauty, in all its unexpected variety, but borderless, undivided, its political lines of separation erased; he had seen the earth, at last, as single, precious, indivisible, irreplaceable.

So maybe it is no bad thing that our return to the bleak weeks of January is also a return to the season and the Sundays of Epiphany.

I can't say that on my holiday I experienced anything quite so spectacular as 'This pendant world, in bigness as a Starr Of smallest Magnitude close by the Moon', as Milton, with astonishing prescience, imagined the view from space.

But I did get a chance to look back from a distance, to have something of an overview and a new perspective. And my holiday did, in its own way, open out a little epiphany that might be a light for me in the dark time of the year.

It was not the earth from space that gave me a glimpse of blue-green beauty, but John Piper's Britten Memorial Window in the parish church in Aldeburgh. There a deep blue, set with a Palmeresque crescent moon, flows down into the three lights, showing in rich colour and detail three scenes: the return of the prodigal, on the left; the three children safe in the burning fiery furnace, on the right; and, in the centre, the sinuous green curves of 'the curlew river', flowing towards us, unbidden, from its hidden source.

So I will set the light and lift of that epiphany against the sluggish gravitation of my return to work. For in my return I see that other return and embrace of the prodigal; I see the hint and glint of an angel with me in the furnace of events; and, flowing between them, free of all January ice, I glimpse a curling, blue-green river of grace.

11

The Apostle and the Poet

There is something a little teasing, a little provoking, in the incongruous meeting, on 25 January, of St Paul and Robert Burns: the apostle and the poet constrained for ever to share the same feast day!

I used to choose between them. One year I'd be pious with St Paul and meditate on that astonishing conversion, and the next I'd forget that his feast had come up and find myself being bibulous instead with Burns. And Burns came first, in my life at least; for my Scottish mother would quote him often and aptly, and not just on Burns Night. She taught me 'The Banks O' Doon' when I was still quite a little boy. I loved to sing that final verse –

> Wi' lightsome heart I pu'd a rose,
> Fu' sweet upon its thorny tree!
> And may fause Luver staw my rose,
> But ah! She left the thorn wi' me.

– though I had to wait until I was a lovelorn teenager to find out what those words meant.

And then, towards the end of that stormy youth, I encountered St Paul, and as I wrestled with Romans, he opened up for me some of the biggest questions and deepest mysteries of life – both mine and the world's.

Now, though, I read them together, and they make strange conversations in my mind. St Paul's powerful thought about our place in the wider creation, about how our fall, our own ruins and failings, have somehow tangled nature herself and ensnared her in our shadow, subjected her to futility, seems all the more pressing in the midst of environmental depredation and climate change.

But that insight had already been sown in my imagination long before I read St Paul, when my mother recited from Burns's poem 'To a Mouse on Turning Her Up in Her Nest With the Plough':

I'm truly sorry Man's dominion
Has broken Nature's social union,
An' justifies that ill opinion,
Which makes thee startle,
At me, thy poor, earth-born companion,
An' fellow-mortal!

The apostle can tell me that the whole creation is groaning, but it is the poet who shows me that truth, in all its minute particularity; shows me the 'sleeket, cowran, tim'rous beastie', through whose nest we have run the ploughshare of our dominion.

Both the poet and the apostle make me feel my deep kinship with all our fellow creatures, make me know that we are all in this together. I feel very keenly the poet's despair; indeed, our present political crisis makes us all too aware that:

Mousie, thou art no thy-lane,
In proving foresight may be vain:
The best laid schemes o' Mice an' Men
Gang aft agley,
An' lea'e us nought but grief an' pain,
For promis'd joy!

But if the poet speaks my grief, the apostle restores my hope.

So with 'the fields laid bare an' waste, An' weary Winter comin' fast', I turn back to St Paul and remember that 'the sufferings of this present time are not worth comparing with the glory about to be revealed to us', when the creation 'will be set free from its bondage to decay'.

Tonight I'll keep the feast for them both, raise a warming glass to a meeting of the spiritual and the spirituous, and be glad that on my study table there is more than one commentary on Romans, but also more than one good dram.

12

In Southwark Cathedral

I was in Southwark last Friday – a borough I venerate as a place of both continuity and renewal. Walking up the High Street towards London Bridge, I glanced down an alley at the George Tavern in its old stable yard, a glorious inn already marked by name in the first known map of Southwark in 1543, and celebrated for all its literary associations in Pete Brown's entertaining book *Shakespeare's Local*. Tempting as it was, there was no time to slip down to the George; for I was on my way to a service at Shakespeare's other local: the parish church where his brother is buried and which has now become a cathedral.

As I passed through the rich sights and scents, the gregarious and multilingual hubbub of Borough Market, I was poignantly aware of that other day, on the eve of Pentecost, when I had walked through that same market minutes before the deadly terrorist attack in 2017. The attack had left Southwark stunned and in lockdown – but not for long. Soon the market was thriving and buzzing again, and the cathedral, which had been cordoned off as a scene of crime, was soon the scene of prayer, comfort and, most of all, resilience and renewal for the community.

The cathedral was certainly buzzing when I got there on Friday. It was, you might say, thick with bishops, resplendent in their white and red rochets and chimeres, the Bishop of London and the Archbishop of Canterbury in their midst. They were all gathered there for the consecration of Andrew Rumsey – a man with whom I once played rock 'n' roll in a band, the Crocodiles – as the new Bishop of Ramsbury. I was there to witness it all and pray for him as he underwent a change in position that was still a continuity of ministry, just as the church we were gathered in had been consecrated as a cathedral but continued, as richly as ever, to be a parochial and local presence.

And if there was anyone there who would share that rich sense of place and locality, it was Rumsey himself, whose excellent book *Parish: An Anglican Theology of Place* celebrates not only these historical continuities but also the radical way Christ stands in our place and stands with us in every place and parish.

I was up in the choir with the visiting clergy, well away from the throng of consecrating bishops, but I heard the long echo of those beautiful words 'To heal, not to hurt, to build up, not to destroy … a faithful steward … with all your household …'

I glanced across the sanctuary at the one bishop who was up there with us, lying comfortably on his back, the fine lawn of his rochet gathered in at the wrist of a hand that was holding the Bible, in whose translation he played such a part. Even in effigy, Bishop Lancelot Andrewes was a central presence for me in that place. The man whose sermons had helped to convert T. S. Eliot, whose work on the Authorized Version had so renewed our language and our faith, would have been glad that the new bishop, who today took the ancient title of Ramsbury, was also a poet and a translator of ancient wisdom into new words.

13

Snowfall

I was in the wood-panelled upper hall of an old college, standing by a blazing log fire and gazing out through diamonded panes, set in a mullioned stone casement, when it started to snow. I watched the snow fall gently, gracefully, seemingly in slow motion; for that first snow was of the best possible kind: large soft flakes drifting slowly down, unhurried, pausing, and even lifting a little with the small eddies and flaws of the wind as they made their long descent.

It was magical, and the two of us in that room, whose conversation was stilled by the sight, both felt that tremor of old excitement and wonder that told us that the child within was still alive and well, as the cloisters and playing fields below us gradually shimmered into whiteness. I called to mind the wonderful and justly famous passage with which Joyce closes the last story in *Dubliners*:

> … snow was general all over Ireland. It was falling softly on every part of the dark central plain, on the treeless hills, falling softly upon the Bog of Allen and, farther westward, softly falling into the dark mutinous Shannon waves. It was falling, too, upon every part of the lonely churchyard where Michael Furey lay buried. It lay thickly drifted on the crooked crosses and headstones, on the spears of the little gate, on the barren thorns. His soul swooned slowly as he heard the snow falling faintly through the universe and faintly falling, like the descent of their last end, upon all the living and the dead.

The supple cadences and inversions of softly falling … falling softly … falling faintly … faintly falling had themselves evoked a kind of slow swoon in my 17-year-old soul when

I first read it, and ever since then that sentence has been a kind of undermusic or motif in my appreciation of snowfall.

Joyce's elegiac tone also touches on something that we all feel when the first snow falls: that falling itself, the gravity of things, the inevitability of descent, is somehow blessed and redeemed by beauty in the gentle fall of snow. It suggests to us the possibility that there might be a letting go that is not calamitous, precipitous, helpless. The American band Over the Rhine have a song, 'Let it Fall' (from the album *Blood Oranges in the Snow*, Great Speckled Dog, 2014), with the refrain:

> Whatever we've lost, I think we're going to let it go, Let it fall, like snow' Cause rain and leaves and snow and tears and stars … They all fall with confidence and grace So let it fall, let it fall …

Such were my musings from the mellowed warmth of a college hall, but when, early the next morning, I descended to the streets and made my way to the bus station, I thought again. For there, curled in a freezing doorway, bundled against the cold in dirty blankets and a torn sleeping bag, was a woman sleeping amid the litter, a strand of her red hair falling across her face, pale white in the reflected light of the snow on the street just beyond her little alcove.

She too must have played in the snow as a child, but I knew that her perspective on last night's snow would have been very different from mine.

Those who have cared enough to campaign against homelessness, those who give what they can, when they can, and who urge us all to make compassionate choices in our politics, have of late been insulted and dismissed as 'snowflakes'; but to my mind, that name should be a badge of honour, a call to come down from on high and to melt with compassion.

14

Cuthbert's Gospel

I am just back from a visit to the British Library's 'Anglo-Saxon Kingdoms' exhibition. I spent the whole afternoon there, but would happily have stayed for a week, standing in the presence of so many moving and beautiful manuscripts about which I had read but never thought I would actually see.

But there they all were, including the Vercelli manuscript that contains *The Dream of the Rood*, the poem spoken by the cross, which is, for me at least, the foundation of all English Christian poetry. It was flanked on one side by the only manuscript of *Beowulf* and on the other by the *Exeter Book*, which contains the enigmatic riddles that so fascinated Tolkien and which he wove into his *legendarium*.

It was a perfect place for the manuscript of *The Dream*; for on the one hand that poem speaks deeply into the heroic world of *Beowulf*, and on the other it is itself a kind of riddle, in which a strange tree tells the story, from its own perspective, of how it discovered that the wounded man whom it bore on its boughs was God Almighty. It is only part way through the poem, which has no title, that the tree reveals itself as 'the rood', the cross of Christ.

But the most moving book of all was the smallest in the exhibition: the St Cuthbert Gospel. A seventh-century manuscript copy of the Gospel of St John, it has an extraordinary aura and presence, not simply because it is the oldest bound book in Europe but because of the saint whose book it was, the long centuries it has endured and the glorious Gospel it contains.

This was the one book that I had seen before, in Durham, which is where it really belongs. I had visited an exhibition there, 'Bound to Last: Bookbinding from the Middle Ages to the Present Day', and had been expecting little more than the beautiful leather tooling and luxury embossing of prestige binders.

And then I came face to face with the St Cuthbert Gospel: the very book that they placed on his breast in his coffin, the Gospel that he loved the most, and lived so fruitfully; a little pocket-book, red-leather-bound and all intact, which had sailed through centuries to meet me there on Palace Green.

And, in that presence, it seemed that every concern for bindings and covers fell away, and that I heard the saint himself, chanting the words that St Augustine heard and that brought him also to the Gospel, *Tolle lege, tolle lege*: take up and read! That experience moved me to write a sonnet, which I published in my collection *Parable and Paradox*, and standing again before that little book yesterday, in London, I called it back to mind:

Cuthbert's Gospel

I stand in awe before this little book,
The Gospel that lay close on Cuthbert's breast,
Its Coptic binding and red leather-work
As sound and beautiful as when they placed
This treasure with the treasure they loved best
And set them sailing through the centuries
Until these coffined riches came to rest
In front of me as open mysteries.

But as I look I seem to hear him speak
'This book is precious but don't waste your breath
On bindings and half uncials and the like,
Breathe in the promise of a better birth
Tolle et lege, try and find it true,
The bound Word waits to be made flesh in you.'

15

In the South Downs

It is extraordinary how often landscape and weather seem to form, between them, a series of perfect expressions for our own inner feelings and intuitions. Things that we could hardly put into words are being said for us in the lift of land as it folds into hill and down, in the way that cloud-shadows move across a field, the way hills shade into blue in the distance. Is it that one's mind goes out as one sees these things and mantles them with meaning? Or is it that to see them at all is to be furnished with a new spaciousness, a new range of possibility in the soul, an 'inscape', as Hopkins called it?

I certainly felt that sense of correspondence between the outer and the inner when I made a journey into Sussex with a friend, and saw the rise of the Downs and smelt the freshness and hint of the sea in the air.

We were returning to the scenes of his childhood, and with a great sense of poignancy and completion; for we had come to return his mother gently to God's good earth, in a woodland burial ground close to his childhood home and to the church where he had worked the hand pump of the little organ (still in its place) while his mother sang in the choir.

At the committal I had read aloud those words in which St Paul too saw the correspondences between outer and inner, between physical and spiritual, and saw in the growth of every seed a sign of hope: 'What is sown is perishable, what is raised is imperishable. It is sown in dishonour, it is raised in glory. It is sown in weakness, it is raised in power. It is sown a physical body, it is raised a spiritual body.'

Afterwards we climbed up beyond the burial ground, up above the church, up on to Clayton Hill, crowned with 'Jack and Jill', its two old windmills, and looked down on the place we had been. And it was there that I suddenly felt the outer scene expressing for us an inner state for which we had no words. Something in the elevation, in the view, in the way we saw the grave at which we had stood from a new perspective; something in the springiness of the turf beneath our feet and the astonishing clarity with which the evening sun picked out the tiniest details, all expressed the otherwise inexpressible.

I found myself remembering the opening lines in Hilaire Belloc's essay 'The Slant off the Land', and they returned to my mind like a thanksgiving, like a prayer:

We live a very little time. Before we have reached the middle of our time perhaps, but not long before, we discover the magnitude of our inheritance. Consider England. How many men, I should like to know, have discovered before thirty what treasures they may work in her air? She magnifies us inwards and outwards; her fields can lead the mind down towards the subtle beginning of things; the tiny iridescence of insects; the play of light upon the facets of a blade of grass. Her skies can lead the mind up infinitely into regions where it seems to expand and fill, no matter what immensities.

16

'Recover'd Greenness'

I am glad that George Herbert's day falls as it does, just at the end of February. Although this February has been unseasonably mild, it's often wintry enough; but it's also just as February turns towards March that we get some glimpse or premonition of spring: a warmer wind; the earth breathing forth her flowers, as January's snowdrops are joined by aconites; and, in their delicate and translucent pinks and rich purples, crocuses open outwards and upwards, spreading their petals to woo the warmer sun that they know is there, even though we sometimes cannot feel it.

I think of this as Herbert's time of year not just because we keep his day on 27 February but because, for me at least, one of his most perfect and most personal poems, 'The Flower', returns to my mind in this season, with its opening exclamation:

> How fresh, oh Lord, how sweet and clean
> Are thy returns! even as the flowers in spring.

It is supremely the poem of return and recovery, as those first returning blossoms in the outer world express, for Herbert, an inner recovery from the experience of depression:

> Who would have thought my shriveled heart
> Could have recovered greenness? It was gone
> Quite underground …

It's not that Herbert doesn't know he will have to go through the cycle of loss and recovery many times in this life; not that he doesn't lament, and long for, that final recovery and resurrection Christ has promised:

Oh that I once past changing were,
Fast in thy Paradise, where no flower can wither!

But still he knows that each of these recoveries keeps the promise and brings its fulfilment a little closer.

This poem also brings a happy memory for me of another poet, and of a day I spent with Seamus Heaney at Little Gidding. It was to this haven, to his friend Nicholas Ferrar, that Herbert had sent the precious manuscript of his poems while he lay dying in Bemerton.

Heaney was there to read Eliot's great poem in the chapel that inspired it, but he was just as happy to revel in its associations with Herbert. Heaney had himself been in hospital and recovered, and at one point he looked at me, with a twinkle in his eye, and spontaneously quoted from Herbert's poem:

And now in age I bud again,
After so many deaths I live and write;
I once more smell the dew and rain,
And relish versing.

I will never forget with what relish he spoke the words 'And relish versing', tasting them on his tongue. And now in age I relish versing too, and offer to Herbert afresh the little sonnet I wrote for him and published in my collection *The Singing Bowl*:

George Herbert

Gentle exemplar, help us in our trials
With all that passed between you and your Lord,
That intimate exchange of frowns and smiles
Which chronicled your love-match with the Word.
Your manuscript, entrusted to a friend,
Has been entrusted now to every soul.
We make a new beginning in your end
And find your broken heart has made us whole.
Time has transplanted you, and you take root,
Past changing in the paradise of Love.
Help me to trace your Temple, tune your lute,
And listen for an echo from above.
Open the window, let me hear you sing,
And see the Word with you in everything.

17

Gladness of the Best

There are particular places – old churches, the studies or writing rooms of great poets, places that have witnessed or absorbed something exceptional – that are, in some sense, resonant, as though the memories they preserved were themselves a kind of sound or music, whose faint traces or vibrations still tingle through the stone and wood to touch the modern pilgrim.

Usually the place is ancient and the resonance is no more than a metaphor. But last Friday I visited just such a place, whose resonance was more than metaphorical, though its history goes back less than a hundred years: I visited the recording studio at Abbey Road.

Even as you approach the place, emerging from the Underground at St John's Wood, the echoes of the Beatles begin, with the kiosk at the Tube station, as full and colourful as those at a Catholic shrine; and by the time you get to the famous zebra crossing, you are aware that many others are taking the same path, just to cross the crossing, to gaze at the studio through the railings and to write their messages of gratitude for that glad music in red felt pens on the long white wall, which is filled to the brim and every three months whitewashed and filled again.

But I was going a little further. By a happy chain of events, I had an appointment to record songs and poems there for the Ordinary Saints Project.

So I found myself in the inner sanctum: Studio 2, where the Beatles recorded every album, including the eponymous masterpiece that made Abbey Road so famous. But I soon realized that the Beatles were only a small part of the resonance of this place. I walked past photographs of Elgar, at the opening of the studio, with his friend George Bernard Shaw; photographs of Glenn Miller and his Orchestra, recording here just before the fatal plane crash; photos of Jacqueline du Pré, looking up from her cello radiant with joy; and, amid them, wonderful pictures of the Beatles in all their varied phases and stages, from cuddly mop-top to transcendental guru.

As he set up the beautiful old Neumann microphones, dating from the 1940s, into which so many of my heroes had sung, the sound engineer told me that, because of the way sound decays, the way it fades, each moment half as much as before, it is theoretically the case that no sound is ever lost entirely; that, somehow, all the music ever made here is still around. Resonance, indeed.

After I had recorded the scheduled poems and songs, I added one more: a new poem, from my sequence in *After Prayer* responding to George Herbert's 'Prayer I'. It reflects on the phrase 'gladness of the best', and it gave me a particular pleasure to record it in this particular place:

Gladness of the best

If prayer itself is gladness of the best,
Then all the best in everything is prayer.
Everything excellent, from east to west,
The best of sacred, best of secular,
The Beatles sing *you know you should be glad*
And that glad song is gladness of the best,
You know you're loved, *you know that can't be bad,*
Your once-lost love is found and you are blessed.
From that exultant sound in Abbey Road
To jubilation in the Albert Hall,
From well-honed phrases, to a well-wrought ode,
Whatsoever things are lovely, all

Brought to the source of every excellence,
That God might give them back as sacraments.

18

Leafing through the Word-Wood

It is easy to denigrate social media; and if we ever take a long view on it, we may conclude that they have done more harm than good. But there are still beautiful things to be found out there, and still people who make original and even counter-intuitive use of the web, posting tweets whose whole purpose is not to get you scrolling down but strolling out instead.

One such is the nature writer Robert Macfarlane, whose book *Landmarks* has done so much to help us treasure, preserve and use the distinctive vocabulary that belongs to each of our distinctive landscapes. Every day he sends out a 'Word of the Day', with some note or illustration that helps to re-enchant both land and language, to turn you outdoors or tempt you to take into your hands a real book and leaf through it.

Today he wrote:

'Library': a treasure-house of books, a sanctuary for study. 'Library' comes from the Latin *liber* meaning both 'book' & 'bark', from the early use of tree-bark as a writing material. As the word's roots tell us, libraries are story-forests, wildwoods of words.

I love the idea of the library as a story-forest, but the linguistic link in *liber* between 'book and bark' took root in me and branched out in all kinds of unexpected ways. I remembered the seat I had in the university library, looking across my desk through a wide window to the lovely branches of a horse chestnut so close that I could imagine myself to be reading in a tree house.

Then I remembered the days when I did just that, climbing trees precariously with my copy of *Treasure Island* in one hand, till the platform on swaying branches where I read became the crow's nest of the *Hispaniola*.

Macfarlane set me thinking too of how, in almost any book I open, idly turning the leaves, I find that I am on the topmost branch of some tree of learning, opening the latest finding of a discipline whose branches go back to the great trunk of all enquiry, and deep into the roots of human curiosity where every science and art has its origin.

Or if I am reading poetry, again I have the same sense, as when Larkin watches the trees coming into leaf and feels that it is 'Like something almost being said'.

Larkin's poignant poem 'The Trees' unfolds from the upper branches of a long tradition of terse, elegiac, limpid verse, which he has fully absorbed and has at his command. The form and rhyme scheme of that quatrain are from Tennyson's *In Memoriam*; their melancholy undertone is as much Hardy's as it is Larkin's, and now, as I read it, it is mine. Perhaps Larkin, as a librarian himself, could hardly help reading the leaves he encountered on his walks, and summoning them afresh, in the greenness of their grief, to relax and spread into the leaves of his poetry book.

But libraries and forests are both under threat, both marginalized in a world driven by the little silicon screens that Macfarlane subverts with his magical posts. I am writing this, as it happens, on World Book Day. Perhaps it should be World Bark Day too, and librarians and naturalists alike could celebrate the twin roots of *liber*.

19

An Unexpected Arrival

I was in the railway station in York, among a group of disconsolate and displaced passengers decanted out of various delayed or diverted trains and left to stew on Platform 3, waiting for replacement services, when something superb and unexpected happened.

I was trying to get back to Cambridge from St Andrews, where I had enjoyed an intense and wonderful few days taking part in a close reading of *Four Quartets*. Indeed, some lines from 'The Dry Salvages' had been going through my head: lines to the effect that we are never the same people at the end of the journey as we were when we left the station, or who 'will arrive at any terminus', when our train stopped suddenly just north of Berwick-upon-Tweed and we were told that there was a broken-down train ahead of us. T. S. Eliot was right: we were going nowhere.

Eventually – in about the time it takes to read and digest Eliot's *Complete Poems* – we limped into York, and I joined that group of other frustrated passengers looking for a fresh connection.

And that is when it happened. We were all looking at our watches, straining at changing departure boards and listening to the scarcely audible garble of announcements, when a train did appear in the distance – but it was not one that any of us expected. With great clouds of white steam, with a glorious whistle sounding above the steady chuff-chuff and the rhythm of its wheels, resplendent in its green and black livery, its brass plates polished and shining, the *Flying Scotsman* came proudly down the line, pulling a couple of old Pullman carriages, and stopped just beyond us with a satisfying sigh of hissing steam.

If the appearance of the train was unexpected and wonderful, the effect it had on the people on that platform was even more so. Suddenly the very same people who had been checking their watches, shouting or scolding into their phones, sighing and frowning and complaining into the air, were all now smiling, standing, exclaiming to one another on how lovely it was, pressing pause on complaint forms or angry emails so as to take photos instead.

I have occasionally happened on platforms scheduled for the arrival of famous steam trains, and then, of course, everyone knows what's coming: the place is crowded with enthusiasts taking photographs and checking numbers. But on this occasion the *Scotsman* had, I imagine, been just as delayed as we were, and no one was expecting its arrival. There was no reception committee; so it all felt unforced, natural, a sheer bonus.

And that is why it had the effect it did. All of us, myself included, were lifted unexpectedly out of our petty little cycles of self-pitying complaint, and forgot ourselves all together for a moment as this shining emblem of a bygone age arrived.

Was it just nostalgia? Partly, perhaps; but I don't think everyone on that platform was necessarily a signed-up steam enthusiast. I think it's partly because the engines of that era were and are, objectively, things of beauty, but mostly because anything that has been loved and cared for, restored from ruin and treasured again, carries with it a kind of aura, a kind of benediction. And that goes for people as well as steam engines.

20

Saying the Names

We are in Northumberland for a few days, staying in Amble, a small fishing port that Maggie and I have been visiting for more than 20 years. When you stand on the jetty in the harbour mouth, where the River Coquet runs into the sea, you can look upstream and see Warkworth Castle – 'this worm-eaten hold of ragged stone', as Shakespeare called it – still standing proud. Amid its ruins my children first played at knights-in-armour.

Or you can turn and look out to sea; and there lies Coquet Island, with the morning light beginning to brighten behind it, as thousands of puffins and roseate terns enjoy their sanctuary there. Though there is a deeper sanctuary still; for the lighthouse rises from the ruins of a monastery, and the island was, for a while, one of St Cuthbert's island hermitages.

But when I first wondered down to this harbour, very early one morning in 1996, it was neither the castle nor the island that drew my attention: it was the little fishing fleet and, more particularly, it was the names of these sturdy vessels that attracted me: *Providence*, *Fidelity* and *Fruitful Bough*, all somehow resonant, redolent, of Prayer Book and Scripture.

As the light strengthened and the tide came in to lift these little ships that morning, 23 years ago, I sensed that there was a poem there, just in the names themselves, and I jotted them down on a scrap of paper. I felt like a jeweller with a purse full of pearls, waiting for the moment to give them the right setting.

Eventually that came; and far from Amble, in landlocked Cambridgeshire, I wrote a poem, 'Saying the Names'. It's 20 years since they kindly published that poem in *The Ambler*,

Amble's community newspaper, but visiting the place again I was delighted to see that many of those boats were still there, crewed by a rising generation; and for old times' sake I went down to admire them in the early-morning light, just as they were when I wrote the opening lines of 'Saying the Names':

Dawn over Amble, and along the coast
Light on the tide flows to Northumberland,
Silvers the scales of herring freshly caught
And gleaming in their boxes on the dock,
Shivers the rainbow sheen on drops of diesel,
And lights at last the North Sea fishing fleet.
Tucked into harbour here, their buoyant lines
Lift to the light on plated prows their names,
The ancient names picked out in this year's paint:
Providence, *Bold Venture*, *Star Divine*
Are first along the quay-side. *Fruitful Bough*
Has stemmed the tides to bring her harvest in.
Orcadian Mist and *Sacred Heart*, *Aspire*,
Their names are numinous, a found poem.

I know that the fishermen of Amble and so many other places have been through many vicissitudes and uncertainties, and for all of us it seems that there is more uncertainty to come; but I took comfort in the continuity of those names not just over the two decades of my visits but from generation to generation, and reaching back into the Scriptures they echo.

And that is how, all those years ago, I ended my poem:

Those Bible-burnished phrases live and lift
Into the brightening tide of morning light
And beg to be recited, chanted out,
For names are incantations, mysteries

Made manifest like ships on the horizon.
Eastward their long line tapers towards dawn
And ends at last with Freedom, Radiant Morn.

21

A Texan Interlude

I am writing this from the Lone Star State, as the Texans love to call it, after speaking at the Dallas diocesan clergy conference. This took place at the diocesan retreat centre which, true to the Texan scale of things, turned out to be an enormous ranch-style complex set in its own grounds, with lakes, pine-forests, stables and horses – and, it goes without saying, a shooting range.

Indeed, my first trip to Texas, some years ago, had made clear to me how different things are here. I remember finding myself sitting nervously in what should have been the driver's seat of a pumped-up pick-up truck, and seeing in the back window of the truck in front of us a gun rack loaded with three rifles. Just below it there were two stickers: one said: 'Don't mess with Texas', the other simply read: 'John 3.16'. I felt that something had been lost in translation.

Though, curiously enough, it was translation – and specifically Cranmer's translations of the Latin Offices into the rich language of the Book of Common Prayer – that provided some common ground on this particular visit. Each morning we concluded matins by reciting the General Thanksgiving together, and even though there were some unfamiliar things in the other Offices, time and again we fell into the familiar cadences and phrases of the Prayer Book.

Over the course of the conference it emerged that we had much else in common: all the usual vicissitudes of parish life and the kinds of things clergy enjoy complaining, commiserating or clashing about when they meet together. But their own distinct challenges came out sharply too: ministry to the huge number of young men, mostly African Americans, who end up incarcerated in Texas; and work with Hispanic and Latino people who are feeling marginalized and threatened in the new political climate. There was a call for more bilingual candidates to come forward for ordination.

The two most popular options for the afternoon off were skeet shooting and a 'High–Low soccer match' between the Anglo-Catholics and the Evangelicals (the Anglo-Catholics won: It seems that Muscular Christianity is differently distributed here). I took neither of these options, but walked instead on the trails through the piney woods – while snakes slithered off the path and turkey buzzards circled above – and reflected on how remarkable it was that the poetry of George Herbert, which was what I was bringing to their table, had as deep a reach and as much power to move and renew the soul in this strange contradictory land as it had in the little parish of Bemerton.

I had been reading 'The Windows' with them. Herbert's account of how, faced with the impossibilities of preaching, one feels like some piece of 'brittle crazie glass', seemed to make as much sense to them in the brittle craziness of their divided society as it does to us in the brittle craziness of ours.

And Herbert's resolution of that dilemma, in the image of stained glass, in the way the story of Christ's life and Passion could be 'annealed' into the fragile glass of our lives, the way the colours of his love and grace might redeem and render translucent our own stains, seemed as vital there as it is here:

Doctrine and life, colours and light, in one
When they combine and mingle, bring
A strong regard and awe; but speech alone
Doth vanish like a flaring thing,
And in the ear, not conscience, ring.

22

'Home Thoughts from Abroad'

I find myself travelling further and more frequently than I ever thought I would – perhaps further than I should – and so I am still on the road as I write this, thinking 'home thoughts from abroad'.

And while I too might sigh with Robert Browning and say, 'Oh, to be in England Now that April's there', it is not only because I too would like to be there 'while the chaffinch sings on the orchard bough' but also because I know through what hideous halts and lurches my country is passing, round what blind bends we race to some unknown end, and it is hard to hear these things belatedly and from afar, to share them only second-hand, and not to feel them along the pulse with my fellow citizens as we pass through this crisis together. By the time I hear *Today*, it's already yesterday.

Of course, travel has its compensations too, its gifts and revelations. Last week I was amid the flat plains and wide skies of Texas, finding that George Herbert still had a place and a voice among the longhorns and the pick-up trucks. Today I am in 'the high dry hallows of Montana', in the little university town of Bozeman: already 5,000 feet above sea level, and circled on all sides by the snow-capped peaks of no fewer than four different mountain ranges. It certainly makes a change from Cambridge.

I'm here to do a poetry reading and to give some lectures on poetry and theology, but before I do that I have a little pilgrimage to make. For it was here, in Bozeman, that my guitar was made. I have a treasured old Gibson J45, on which I have composed almost all my songs, into whose hollows I have poured so much of my own feelings and from whose soundboard has come a rich music that owed more to the quality of the guitar than the skill of the player.

Some years after I had acquired this guitar I read an article about how Gibson made them in Montana because the altitude and the dry air were perfect for curing the wood, and because in this rugged part of the States there was still a tradition of craftsmanship, of working slowly and patiently in wood, taking pains and care over the shaping and finishing of a well-wrought work.

Inspired by that article, and by the paradox that the shaped emptiness of the sound box is what gives the guitar its fullness and voice, I wrote a sonnet about my guitar; now, at last, I shall have a chance to read it in the place it celebrates:

Hollows

I lift you lightly, you were made for me;
No box of rain to give the grateful dead,
But breath instead and beauty for the living.
A certain shaping of the mountain air
Censes its gentle wood-scent in your hollows.
The high, dry, hollows of Montana
First saw you braced and fretted, resonant
And ready to be sounded into song.
The smallest tremor trembles through your form
And turns the air to music. My full heart
Is poured into your forming emptiness
And given back as passion for another,
Your hollows hold a weight that sets me free.
I lift you lightly, you were made for me.

23

Rolling Away the Stone

Holy Saturday is a strange, in-between day. I've heard it described as the day we all hold our breath, poised between the grief of Good Friday and the hope of Easter.

But I think it would be truer to say that it is the day when heaven holds our breath. For on Good Friday we see Christ, the second Adam, breathing his last breath, and ours, and entrusting it to heaven for safe keeping. And that breath is held in heaven till he releases it afresh and renews us on Easter Day, when he breathes on us and says, 'Receive the Holy Spirit.' But over the waiting space of Holy Saturday there is a breathless hush.

We have our activities, of course: the children coming to make Easter gardens while others decorate the church; and for the more disorganized among us there is the sudden realization that Easter eggs are still to be bought.

I always try to find time, though, somewhere on that day, for a decent walk. Likely as not the weather has been rainy, and I soon find my feet stuck in the miry clay, something pulling me earthward even as the birds sing overhead.

On Holy Saturday a couple of years ago I headed into the woods with the dogs, seeking to clear my mind after an exhausting and exacting few weeks of life and ministry. I set out feeling burdened, feeling I scarcely had the imaginative energy left to participate in this great re-enactment and celebration of the drama of our salvation.

For some reason, as a tinny and annoying background to more melancholy thoughts, I had Mott The Hoople's catchy 1973 hit 'Roll Away the Stone' running round in my head. It is not a great work of art. Indeed, some might say they had no business borrowing a gospel image to boost the chorus of a cheesy chat-up song, replete with lines like 'We still got a chance Baby in love and sweet romance.'

And yet in spite of that, as I emerged from the thick of thickets, both outer and inner, and sensed the growing light behind grey clouds, on that tired Holy Saturday the mystery of Easter opened up to me again, and even Mott The Hoople's little chorus was lifted into meaning.

I went home and composed, in the last light of Saturday, a villanelle for Sunday:

As though some heavy stone were rolled away,
You find an open door where all was closed,
Wide as an empty tomb on Easter Day.
Lost in your own dark wood, alone, astray,
You pause, as though some secret were disclosed,
As though some heavy stone were rolled away.
You glimpse the sky above you, wan and grey,
Wide through these shadowed branches interposed,
Wide as an empty tomb on Easter Day.
Perhaps there's light enough to find your way,
For now the tangled wood feels less enclosed,
As though some heavy stone were rolled away.
You lift your feet out of the miry clay
And seek the light in which you once reposed,
Wide as an empty tomb on Easter Day.
And then Love calls your name, you hear Him say:
The way is open, death has been deposed,
As though some heavy stone were rolled away,
And you are free at last on Easter Day.

24

A House of Prayer

I was in the vestry in Norwich Cathedral, preparing to speak at a Holy Week service, when the deacon came in and said, 'Notre-Dame is burning.' We had two minutes to go before our own service – time for a prayer but no time to check the news – and out we went, processing down the long and beautiful nave under the vaulted arches and into the resplendent beauty, the forest of stone and light, that is a great medieval cathedral, to set it ringing again with the prayer and liturgy for which it was built.

When, in the intercessions, the deacon said that Notre-Dame was on fire, and asked for prayers for the firefighters and all the people of France, there was an audible gasp, a physically discernible wave of sympathy and shock as the congregation of one cathedral felt, and knew in their hearts, what it must be like for the congregation of another.

People glanced up at the delicate stone tracery, the intricately carved roof bosses, as though to reassure themselves that they were all still there. Then we entered into the mysteries of the Eucharist, with its anamnesis of death and resurrection, of catastrophic loss and astonishing renewal.

Our Gospel text that evening was St Luke's account of Jesus' looking down over Jerusalem with tears in his eyes, already foreseeing the tragedy of destruction, not one stone left on another. I led a reflection on those tears, drawing on my poem 'Jesus Weeps':

Jesus comes near and he beholds the city
And looks on us with tears in his eyes,
And wells of mercy, streams of love and pity
Flow from the fountain whence all things arise.

And on that evening I had the sense of how, in Christ, God enters deeply into our tragic condition, weeping with us not only for the loss of those we love, as he wept for Lazarus, not only for our moral calamities, which he has come to redeem, but also for our communal and civil losses, when not one beloved stone is left on another, and so for the people of Paris

The next evening we gathered again, relieved to know that, against all expectation, so much of the stonework and, miraculously, the rose window had survived. Our focus that evening was the cleansing of the Temple. Here was a much-needed counterpoint, a deep reminder of the true purpose of every sacred place.

Much has been written of Notre-Dame as a cultural icon and rightly so, but it is primarily, as Jesus said of the Temple, a house of prayer. And the extraordinary thing is that, even as fierce clusters of flame grew and blossomed up the spire, even as that spire fell, the response of the crowd kindled and flowered into prayer, as people raised their hands and sang hymns. Flames leapt from arch to arch and the house of prayer burned, but prayer itself leapt from the building to the streets, from the stones to the people.

Whatever becomes of our mortal houses, or even of these mortal bodies, prayer itself will burn the stronger. 'Destroy this Temple and I will raise it in three days', Jesus said, to the great scandal of those who keep the outer stones; but Easter proved him as good as his word, and the temple of his risen body, which is our real house of prayer, will outlast even the greatest cathedral.

25

Going, Going?

The other week Maggie and I took the chance of an untrammelled day together and made a leisurely progress down the Stour Valley, exploring the lovely string of little towns and villages from Clare, through Cavendish to Melton, and then across to Lavenham.

As we took pleasure in the pargetting patterned on the plaster walls of country cottages, in the timbered frames of medieval weavers' houses and guildhalls, in the old pubs, the village greens, the light airy churches, their feathery fan tracery and lucid Gothic arches reaching up beneath the blue April skies, I found myself recalling that listing litany in Larkin's poem 'Going, Going', conjuring up the meadows and the lanes, 'The guildhalls, the carved choirs …'.

Of course, as his title suggests, Larkin's tone is elegiac, even despairing: he felt that it was all going, all being pulled down and 'bricked in', that it wouldn't outlast the poet himself. Yet here we were, 35 years after Larkin's death, and while many beautiful things may still be 'going, going', thank God many are not yet gone.

Although the guildhalls and the carved choirs have survived longer than Larkin expected, he was a more accurate prophet when it came to nature. Famously in that poem, a piece of eco-writing before its time, he begins to doubt the resilience of nature in the face of our onslaught, no longer trusting that the earth will always respond, however we 'mess it about'.

We came home from the Stour Valley to the news of wildfires in the record-breaking Easter heat, and of the climate-change protests, presented on the bulletin as though they were separate items. Again I remembered Larkin's premonition 'That it isn't going to last …'.

Yet something I learned that day in the guildhall in Lavenham gave me hope. Curiously enough, what preserved such a wonderful cluster of medieval buildings for the admiration and pleasure of a later age was not foresight but failure.

The guildhall was built as a crowning glory with the wealth generated by the wool trade, and especially the weaving and dyeing that had made 'Lavenham Blue' famous throughout Europe; but then technology changed, new styles came in, and the people of Lavenham were soon too poor to pull down and remodel their buildings as the fashions changed, as brick and tiles came in and timber and thatch were dismissed as crude country cousins. They were too poor, even, to cover their timbered houses with fashionable façades; so they had to make do and mend, to keep patching up what they had. But then the time came when people remembered the old ways and the old buildings, delighting in them again, and Lavenham's shame became its splendour.

I wondered whether we who have failed in foresight might also be saved by failure; whether the faltering of our heavier industries, the changes in fashion and demand, might return us too to older ways; whether that willingness to make do and mend, which was once the badge of poverty, might soon be celebrated rather than despised, and the old ways might be as much sought after as the old timber houses, 'The guildhall, the carved choirs', which are the glory of England.

26

From One May to Another

On May Day I was out walking in warm sunshine up Rivey Hill with our two greyhounds, George and Zara, ascending a grassy track towards the high ridge and then down through the delicious shade of the greenwood, carpeted with bluebells and fresh with the tender green of newly opened leaves.

For a person habituated to the flatlands of Cambridge, it's wonderful to have a hill at all, and I rested on the bench at the top to gaze down at Linton, nestled in its fold in the Granta Valley. May has come in already rich and full: 'Everything is in delightful forwardness: the violets are not withered before the peeping of the first rose', as Keats wrote to his brother George on a similarly fine day in early May.

Keats has been much in my mind as April turned to May this year, for it was exactly 200 years ago, as April turned to May in 1819, that the finest blossom of his poetry, in that *annus mirabilis*, miraculously unfolded, and the two great odes, the 'Nightingale' and the 'Grecian Urn', flowered into being – not the 'transitory blossom' of the hedges 'white with May', as T. S. Eliot named them, but a flowering that turned eternal, even as it lamented transience.

I am savouring those odes again on their anniversary days, and likewise all the rich letters he wrote alongside them. While I was ascending the hill on 1 May 2019, Keats, on his 1819 May Day, was writing to his sister: 'O there is nothing like fine weather … and, please heaven, a little claret-wine cool out of a cellar a mile deep – with a few or a good many ratafia cakes – a rocky basin to bathe in, a strawberry bed to say your prayers to Flora in …'.

His words echo the verse he'd begun to sketch out the day before:

O, for a draft of vintage! That hath been
Cool'd a long age in the deep-delved earth,
Tasting of Flora and the country green …

Keats's housemate, Charles Brown, was generous with his wine, but never can generosity with the transient have been so rewarded with the permanent, or such a compliment paid to a host on his wine, as when the claret carried up from the damp little cellar in the house at Wentworth Place became that immortal 'draft of vintage', and a basement in Hampstead became the archetype of all cellars: dark and cool 'in the deep-delved earth'.

I say 'never' but that's not quite true. As we enjoy our Eastertide Eucharists in this season of recovery, we do indeed continually exchange the transient for the permanent, and enjoy a draft of vintage full of far more than 'the warm south', for it is full of Life Himself.

This time last year I was asked by my friend Lancia Smith to write a spring blessing for her online journal *Cultivating*, and it came out like this, with a nod not to Keats but to Shelley:

Spring

With each unfolding seed, with every spring,
He breathes the rumour of his resurrection,
As birdsong calls your hidden heart to sing.
So may this season be his benediction,
To lift your love, and bid your prayer take wing,
To thaw your frozen hope, to warm your mind,
For spring has come! Can Heaven be far behind?

27

Touching the Hem

Girton, my college, is beginning to build up to its peculiar exam-term intensity. The buzz of conversation usually to be heard in the college 'social hub' café has gradually quietened, as students hunch over laptops rather than chat to friends; now, in the near silence, there is just the faint patter of keys on keyboards and the almost audible hum of unwonted concentration.

Even those who are tempted by more kindly weather to venture out all take a book with them as they wander into the college gardens or the orchard, which is rich in May with buttercups and daisies sprinkling the grass, and apple, pear and plum trees blossoming above.

But most students are not to be seen in the café, corridors or gardens but are in serried rows in the library or huddled over desks in their rooms.

It can be a little over-intense for some, and I have taken to advertising late-night compline as a kind of chill-out zone: 'Take some space: unwind at the end of a hectic day. Be still for 20 minutes in the candlelight. No demands. No sermon.'

And so I try to tempt them out of the library and the study rooms to unwind a little and bathe their minds in 20 minutes of soothing plainchant. You can see them start to relax as the words of the Office hymn, sung beautifully by the choir, float over them:

> Before the ending of the day,
> Creator of the world, we pray,
> That with thy wonted favour thou
> Wouldst be our guard and keeper now …

And it seems to be helpful for quite a few of them. Of course, I know that liturgy can and should be so much more than a stress-buster, but maybe, for those who do find themselves gradually de-stressed as they bathe in the sound of *Te lucis ante terminum*, the whole experience is in some way a touching of the hem of Christ's garment: something has been given, something disclosed. And the person holding a candle at compline may hear a call, and make a journey, as another stressed woman once did, from touching the hem of Christ's garment to meeting him face to face.

Were we in a monastery and not a college, compline would be followed by the Greater Silence – and indeed some of our students do return to the silence of the library, though not perhaps the deeper silence of the soul.

But for those who wish, compline at Girton is followed not by silence but, in true Cambridge style, an invitation from the chaplain to port and conversation. Sometimes the conversation turns on the music we've just sung or heard, sometimes on the events and stresses of the term; but just occasionally it opens into deeper things, on to more ultimate questions. Just occasionally there is an opening of heart and soul, which in some sense the liturgy itself has made possible; and then it is that, just sometimes, someone takes a few more steps on that journey from the hem of his garment to the light of his countenance.

28

A Little Freshet

Yesterday morning, as I wrote, I sat in the little garden of Ty Pren, a wooden hut, formerly a hermit's cell, gazing out at the beautiful, enigmatic but always enticing outline of Bardsey Island, Ynys Enlli: the Island of Saints. Bees hummed amid the daisies in the hermitage garden, and beyond its low turf walls, which formed a small windbreak and haven, cloud-shadows raced across the grassy fields that slope down to low black cliffs, dropping into the cold sea that surges between the end of the Llyn Peninsula and the holy island.

I was the guest of the present tenant of that little hut, Fraser Paterson, a gardener and artist, and was there to meet him and Claire Henderson Davis, the choreographer and theologian who had once set my Passion sonnets to dance and music.

Now she was working on a new piece, *All Creation Waits*, set on the peninsula here and reimagining the story of the awakenings of Francis and Clare – not as they had happened in Assisi but as though they were happening now; as though Francis and Clare were our contemporaries, young people awakening to the peril of climate change, joining the Extinction Rebellion, seeking not just to commune more intimately with nature but also to hear her voice, and the voice of her Creator, and let them awaken and convert us now.

On that May morning, as we discussed how her project might unfold and what kind of texts I might write for it, it would have been easy to stay in the haven, to luxuriate in that little turf-walled garden, to delight in a sense of unspoilt nature, to indulge in a little nostalgia for the Celtic saints.

But even as we began to plan the project, our conversation was drowned by the thunder of a low-flying jet, roaring in from the Valley airbase in Anglesey. When the last echo was gone and peace seemed to be restored, I remembered at last the poem that had been haunting me, just below the verge of memory, as we had made the journey down the peninsula: a poem by the sometime Vicar of Aberdaron, in whose parish we were, and who thought of this peninsula as a delicate bough, a bough that might break.

R. S. Thomas's poem 'Retirement' seemed more pertinent than ever; for he too had reflected on the fragility of our peace, a 'rare peace' suspended, like civilization, over an abyss into which we might fall at any moment.

Later, guided by Fraser, we ourselves, quite literally, 'crawled out at last' as far as we dared, down the last slopes of the peninsula, then dropping down a perilous descent on slippery steps cut roughly into the black rock, to edge our way on wave-washed stone to find Ffynnon Fair, St Mary's Well, one of the most sacred places in Wales: the little triangular cleft in the rocks into which, miraculously, amid all the brackish tidal pools, sweet fresh water rises, a last refreshment for weary pilgrims before they come to 'the Gate of Paradise' at Bardsey.

I had been looking for an emblem of the little freshet of hope we have, against the rising tide of so much catastrophe, and as Fraser stooped to cup fresh water in his hands at St Mary's Well, I thought that, perhaps, I had found it.

29

Tacking

My little sailing canoe, *Willow,* is back on the water, but this time I'm keeping her on the river Cam near Waterbeach. It's a very quiet part of the river, at least on weekdays, and once I've slipped out in *Willow* and worked my way up the stretch towards Bottisham Lock, then it's just me and the wonderful array of bird life that haunts this lower edge of fenland.

Over the last weeks I have watched a family of coots: the proud mother, in her distinct black coat with its white beak and shield, out with her chicks, still in their orange fluff but growing more confident in the water week by week. When I see her I'm inevitably taken to my childhood memories of reading Arthur Ransom's *Coot Club* and the children's heroic adventures to defend the coot's nest from the 'hullabaloos' in their motorboat, and keep mother and chick together.

Leaving the coot's appealingly untidy nest and tacking over to the other side, I came close to a more magnificent swan's nest, with brooding swan in place, and veered away again so as not to disturb her. This new tack brought me into the path of a great crested grebe, its perky crest feathers giving it the debonair feel, the studied disorder, of a young punk showing off a new tufty haircut.

I'm sure it's very unscientific, but it's difficult not to see distinct personalities in the distinct appearances of different birds. To give the perfect end to my morning's sail, I heard, clear from the cluster of trees beyond the towpath, distinct on that late May morning, my first cuckoo.

How was I so fortunate to have seen and heard so many lovely birds on one brief sail? Well, of course, the fact that I was *sailing* helped: it was a still, quiet morning, and there was no noise or smell of an engine to disturb the wildlife.

And in slender little *Willow* I was low in the water, almost under eye level with the swans and just at the right level to glimpse the nests and sense the scurry of the coot chicks among the reeds as I got close to each bank.

And the fact that I was sailing came into that too. The wind tends to blow up or down the course of the river, which means that while you might have a glorious run before the wind in one direction, you will have to tack against it in the other, so that you've no sooner set your sail on one tack than you're almost bumping into the bank and have to go about and tack to the other bank and so on, zig-zagging slowly up the river.

Of course, there are more efficient ways to travel, but I was here to escape the tyranny of the efficient, to find in self-imposed constraint a series of new serendipities.

In that way sailing is a little like verse-making, perhaps a little like liturgy: I sail my craft up the current of language, tacking back and forth, in iambic pentameters, the five-stress line, and as each line nears its limit I approach the bank of my verse and veer around, for another five-beat stretch.

But just as tacking up this little narrow stretch of the Cam brought me close to the coots and the swans and the grebe, so too the self-chosen constraint of my verse form sometimes reveals little beauties that the plain and efficient motorboat of prose might miss.

30

Making Ripples

A favourite pause on my early-morning walk with our two sagacious greyhounds, George and Zara, is on the little walkway over the ford at Linton. From there I can gaze upstream across the ford at the wide millpond that once served the watermill here.

An elegant bough from a neighbouring tree hangs over it, almost perfectly reflected in the water. I say 'almost' because the pond is never absolutely still: there is always a slight and beautifully varied ripple pattern sent out and widening through the pool from the two silver veils of water that spill over from the top of the old sluice gate at the far end, whose slight motion and murmuring sound make a nice balance with the general stillness and peace of the scene. On this particular morning I found myself focusing more on the ripples than the reflection; for ripples had been recently on my mind.

As part of our 150th anniversary celebrations at Girton we have been looking back at some of the heroic alumnae of our pioneering days. One of those was Hertha Ayrton, the brilliant mathematician, scientist, inventor and suffragette, whose important discoveries were read out to the Royal Society. But although she was proposed as a Fellow in 1902, she was barred by a decree of their council that married women were not eligible to be Fellows. Now Girton has Fellowships named in her honour.

Her pioneering work on electric arcs and on ripples in sand and water is still vital to science in those fields, and I had been reading some extracts that seemed to me as full of poetry as they were of science, especially this passage, written in 1904: 'a single ripple, existing alone, in otherwise smooth sand, initiates a ripple on either side of it … each of these ripples produces another on its farther side – these in turn originate on their farther sides, and so on, till the whole sand is ripple-marked.'

As the ripples ran out over Linton's little millpond, I reflected on how the influence of pioneers such as Hertha, once made to feel so marginal, had rippled out so far; and later that day I wrote a poem for her, which was also inspired by a tapestry being made in her memory by the artist Yelena Popova. The tapestry will soon be unveiled in the community centre at Eddington: a beautiful pattern that combines arcs, waves and ripples. The poem to go with it goes like this:

Ripple-Marked Radiance

They tried to make her think she was alone,
A bright mind on the wrong side of the gap,
But she knew otherwise, and turned the flow
And current of her time to a new light.
Her energy was gathered at an edge;
Potential energy held back awhile,
By the dark gap that prejudice engendered.
Her radiant mind would not be held apart,
But arced across that gap, a sudden blaze
Of genius, invention, and ideas,
Whose ripples still run free in all of us.

Now Hertha Ayrton has herself become
That 'single ripple which initiates
A ripple either side'. Those ripples still
Originate yet further ripples, till
The whole is ripple-marked and radiant.
And we, who gather here remembering her,

Are woven with her in one tapestry,
No longer lone or lonely, but renewed,
Enlarged, and centred in community.

31

The Heart-Language of an Old Dial

I was idly turning the pages of my well-worn Everyman edition of Lamb's *Essays of Elia* when I came upon his essay on 'The Old Benchers of the Inner Temple': the retired lawyers and judges who had perambulated the Inns of Court, especially the Inner Temple, when Lamb was growing up there as a child.

Naturally there are some wonderful pen-portraits of full-blown, late-eighteenth-century eccentricity, force and presence, as in the description of one Thomas Coventry, 'whose person was a quadrate, his step massy and elephantine, his face square as the lion's, his gait peremptory and path-keeping, indivertible from his way as a moving column, the scarecrow of his inferiors, the brow-beater of equals and superiors, who made a solitude of children wherever he came, for they fled his insufferable presence, as they would have shunned an Elisha bear'.

I've met a few dons like that.

It was not the description of the 'benchers' themselves that caught my eye this time but, early in the essay, a beautifully drawn contrast between the old sundials that adorned those courts and the mere mechanism of a clock. The sundials 'take their revelation of time's flight immediately from heaven, holding correspondence with the fountain of light!' And Lamb remembers watching the shadow of the dial as a child: 'How would the dark lines steal imperceptibly on, watched by the eye of childhood, eager to detect its movement, never catched, nice as an evanescent cloud, or the first arrests of sleep!'

But, by contrast, he writes: 'What a dead thing is a clock, with its ponderous embowelments of lead and brass, its pert or solemn dullness of communication, compared with a simple altar-like structure, and silent heart language of the old dial!'

I wonder what further contrasts Lamb would have made with our digital time-keeping. We had already stepped away from reality when mechanical clocks 'quantized' time (as the scientists like to say) – that is to say, artificially divided it up into equally portioned minutes and seconds, doled out indifferently, without consideration either of the movements of the heavens or the movements of the heart. And now we all carry devices that count down milliseconds and intrude on our reveries with inhuman squawks and bleeps.

But sundials keep a truer time: instead of hurrying us on they invite us to linger and read their inscriptions. There is gentle humour in the most famous one: *Horas non numero nisi serenas* ('I count only the sunny hours'). While the course of time is not suspended by the covering of a cloud, there is some wisdom in counting only the serene hours, instead of letting digital countdowns on smartphones take away our serenity.

Hilaire Belloc had a good line in sundial inscriptions, and while he's most remembered for such glorious put-downs as 'I am a sundial, and I make a botch Of what is done far better by a watch', he also had a sense that the sundial keeps soul-time. Perhaps he too was remembering Lamb's essay, with its 'correspondence with the fountain of light', its 'heart language' and its 'dark lines stealing imperceptibly', when he wrote this inscription for a sundial, lost in a forgotten glade, still keeping the time unnoticed, marking, like our inmost soul, 'The Dawn, the Noon, the coming of the Dark'.

Perhaps a little time contemplating neglected sundials might also awaken a neglected soul.

32

A Bridge in the Mist

Not long ago I found myself joining a little pilgrimage along
the banks of the Firth of Forth, through the mist and mizzle
– the haar, as the Scots call the sea-fret that so often covers
the Firth – to the ancient Parish Church of St Cuthbert,
Dalmeny, by South Queensferry, just near where the three
great bridges cross the Firth. I had been in awe of our
glimpses through that mist of the newest of those bridges as
we descended towards the church, its single span held above
the water by delicate strands of cable, fanned and tensed and
taut, like the strings of a harp.

I had come to Edinburgh to speak to a group of Christians
who were spending a few days building bridges of their
own, between their faith and the art of poetry. I had spoken
the day before, in the parish church at Newhaven, about
Shakespeare, and in particular about his beautiful account
of poetry in *A Midsummer Night's Dream* – that passage that
speaks of the way poetry builds a bridge between visible and
the invisible, the way imagination 'apprehends more than
cool reason ever comprehends', how it 'glances from heaven
to earth, from earth to heaven', 'bodies forth the form of
things unknown' and 'gives to airy nothing, a local habitation and a name'.

We had reflected together on the way Shakespeare's
account of poetry so closely parallels St John's account of the
incarnation, in which the Word himself, the very heart and
meaning of heaven, chooses to be bodied forth, to be made
flesh in Christ, to have a local habitation, to take a name.

Now we had ourselves come to a local habitation in
Dalmeny, wonderfully shaped and sculpted in the twelfth
century, to provide a place of worship for the pilgrims who

gathered to cross the Queens ferry on their way to the shrine at St Andrews. We were gathered to share the sacrament in that place, where the ferry, once provided by the saintly Queen Margaret of Scotland, had been replaced by that beautiful new bridge, recently opened by our own Queen Elizabeth.

There was an extraordinary moment when, just before she began the Eucharistic Prayer, the celebrant recited a poem that Jackie Kay, the current makar (poet laureate) of Scotland, had recited on the day that the new bridge was opened. She too had compared the bridge to a harp, and then, in a wonderful simile, saw it:

> Like a great cormorant, perfectly still,
> And lifting your wings out to dry,
> In snell winds or high,
> Come driving rain, come shine …

Her poem expressed just what we had seen ourselves on that misty rainy day: the great, strong, delicate structure:

> here one minute, gone another,
> in the dreich mist, in the haar,
> in the twilight …

I delighted in those piercing and expressive Scots weather-words 'snell' and 'dreich', recited for us in the strong accent that suited them best, but was even more moved by an insight towards the end of the poem:

> the urge to build bridges runs deeper
> than the great rivers they ford.

The poem flowed seamlessly into the more familiar and all-changing words of the Eucharistic Prayer as, once more, the great bridge-builder bridged the gap between heaven and earth, made the crossing for us and was bodied forth again, here by the Firth of Forth, in bread and wine.

33

Tales from the Orchard

One of the best features of our 150th anniversary year at Girton has been a series of tree-planting ceremonies. We have made five new honorary Fellows, all distinguished alumnae, and each of them, from a Japanese princess to a brilliant comedian, has come to our old orchard and planted a new tree.

The ceremonies themselves were entertaining and some-times revealed hidden talents in our new Fellows. Sandi Toksvig, for example, handled a spade with great gusto and took to filling in and watering with as much zeal for the orchard as for the ceremony. But the great thing, from my perspective, was the talk about the orchard itself, given by Dr Roland Randall, a geography Fellow and farmer who has a special care for our orchard and its history. We have rare old trees with wonderful names such as 'Norfolk Beefing', but a favourite of mine is a Victorian variety, 'Gascoyne's Scarlet', and it was from Dr Randall that I learned its history. It was, he said:

A high-quality dessert apple, often said to be a gentlemen's after-dinner dessert apple, which has been grafted high on to one of our old Bramley Seedling trees. It is named after its developer, Mr Gascoyne of Bapchild, near Sitting-bourne, who bred it before 1871 … The apple is large, and harvested in October, just in time for use in the Michael-mas term. One wonders who might have carried out the graft, and who the gentlemen were, to be entertained …

I wondered whether Mr Gascoyne ever knew that his 'gentlemen's apple' was being enjoyed by the young ladies at the newly founded college, referred to by its opponents in his day as 'that infidel place', and I enjoyed the speculation about who might have been invited to enjoy it with them.

But there was more to the story than that. Our tree had flourished so well because it had been grafted high on to a Bramley, already deeply rooted and flourishing, and that Bramley seedling itself had a history, which, appropriately for Girton, began with a woman.

The first known example was grown by Miss Mary Anne Brailsford and planted in Garden Street, Southwell, Nottinghamshire, in the first decade of the nineteenth century, where the tree later belonged to Mr Bramley, the local butcher. The original Bramley tree blew down in a storm in the early 1900s, but a branch grew up from the old trunk and still survives and fruits.

I loved the thought that our gentlemen's after-dinner apple was grafted on to a tree that itself had sprung from a branch that survived a storm as the twentieth century began.

When Girton came to Cambridge, they must have felt like a lost branch being restored, grafted on to the stock of an ancient seat of learning, sustained by it and yet bringing it new fruit and flavour. And I thought too, as I heard this tale, of that other grafting of which St Paul speaks, of how the flourishing of Christianity depended on the sheer grace of its being grafted on to the deep-rooted stock of Israel's ancient faith.

Learning a little more about our orchard also summoned lines from my own poem 'O Radix' with a new vigour:

Now we have need of You, forgotten Root
The stock and stem of every living thing
Whom once we worshipped in the sacred grove,
For now is winter, now is withering
Unless we let you root us deep within,
Under the ground of being, graft us in.

34

Holding an Old Briar Pipe

Occasionally the pleasures of childhood survive and even blossom in adulthood, but in another form. So, with me, there is a kinship between the pleasure I have in handling briar pipes and the pleasure I had in finding conkers.

It wasn't the conker competitions that I enjoyed, standing there at the risk of having one's thumb struck by an opponent's vicious swipe. No, it was picking up the conkers themselves that gave me the greatest pleasure. I loved the swirls and patterns in their shiny brown sides, like the grain in highly polished wood. I especially liked to take a new one out from its fresh green carapace, and to think, as I uncovered it, 'I am the first person ever to see this.'

Now, likewise, I enjoy the patterning on this old Peterson pipe. The stem joins the bowl with a bright silver band, beneath which is the tightly patterned grain of the briar, parts like flames and tiger-stripes, others in tight little knots and whorls, which aficionados call 'bird's-eye'. But unlike the conkers, which soon clouded, dried and shrivelled, my briar pipes stay beautiful. Indeed, their pattern seems enriched by the passing years, aided by all the reading, conversation and writing they have witnessed. This Peterson is a case in point.

About ten years ago I walked out to Grantchester with a couple of American C. S. Lewis scholars, and, over tea in the orchard, they got out their pipes and we began to talk poetry. I was distressed to find I hadn't brought my pipe, but one of my companions produced a 'spare' for me to smoke: a beautiful, large-bowled, long-stemmed Peterson. As I took it up, I noticed from the hallmark on the silver band that it was an early one.

'Why, this is a "pre-Republic Peterson"!' I said, and so it was. So as we smoked we began to think of all the great poetry written in Ireland since this pipe had first been made in Dublin: we recited Yeats and Kavanagh, Longley, Mahon and Heaney – it was wonderful. As we got ready to leave, I gave back the pipe.

'No', said my friend. 'You must keep it; for you know what it is and what it means.'

I demurred, but he insisted. He said: 'I too was given this pipe. I saw it in the Peterson shop in Dublin, and couldn't afford it, but an older and wealthier friend bought it for me.'

Five years later I was leading a retreat about Lewis on the Isle of Wight, and a group of us were smoking pipes in the evening on a balcony looking out over the sea. I took out this pipe and it was much admired; so I told the story. All the while an elderly American, who was co-hosting the event, was grinning from ear to ear. 'Show it to me', he said. 'Yes,' he declared, with some satisfaction, 'I bought this pipe many years ago, and gave it to the man who gave it to you!'

'Then it must come back to you', I said. 'On the contrary', he replied. 'You must keep it, and pass it on, when the time comes, to some younger enthusiast who also knows what it is and what it means.'

I feel certain that that will happen: that the pipe, rather like a wand in *Harry Potter*, will find its next true keeper. I look forward to that day; for the pipe will carry with it all the good talk, good stories and poetry that it has already encouraged, and, in new hands, be ready for more.

35

Motes

There is always a special frisson, a little tremor of magic, when the invisible is made visible, when the hidden, the taken-for-granted, is suddenly revealed and resplendent.

And yet it is also an everyday occurrence, at least if one's eyes are open. Take, for example, the dust in my cluttered room. It's always there, suspended in the air, but it remains, for the most part, invisible and unremarked, floating, moving, secretly marking the subtle currents of the air.

But when a cloud uncovers the sun, and a single shaft of light shines through on to my desk to make a bright splash on the pages of an open book, then, suddenly, I perceive that the air through which it falls is full of dance and move-ment: the little motes of dust, moving in and out of its beam, shine out as tiny stars that lift and fall in whorls and swirls, like the star-forming nebulae so beautifully revealed by the Hubble Space Telescope; the unseen suddenly appears, like the thoughts and lines that rise into the light of one's mind from the unknown and the unconscious.

When I first saw these swirls of suddenly illumined dust, as a child, I imagined them as stars and galaxies, and thrilled to the change in scale. So I was glad to discover that I was not the only one to have thought this, when I came across Micheal O'Siadhail's beautiful poem 'Cosmos', which com-pares God's creation of our subtly unfolding cosmos to the unfolding of themes and variations by a jazz maestro. Set in a jazz club in New Orleans, the poem opens with a vivid image of 'a spotlight tunnels dust in its beam.'

When the trumpeter warms to his solo, the poet reim-agines the original act of creation itself and reimagines the swarms of dust in the spotlight as 'swirls of galaxies'.

A while back, when I was working on the last pieces for my 2019 poetry collection *After Prayer*, there was a moment when one of those sudden shafts of spring sunlight brought its illumination, and I tried to express something of what it made me feel in a little poem for that collection, 'Motes', recalling O'Siadhail on the one hand, and George Herbert on the other (with a little nod to Donne).

Because *After Prayer* is, in part, a response to Herbert, I thought I would try using some of the beautiful forms and verse patterns he invented. This little poem follows the metrical pattern and rhyme-scheme of Herbert's poem 'The Pulley'; but whereas Herbert's poem is about being pulled back up to heaven by our own weariness, mine is about how, in moments of quiet and completion, the breath of heaven seems to stir, and its light to illumine even the dust of this world.

Motes

In stillness after prayer
A shaft of sunlight finds my quiet room,
Where motes of dust are dancing in the air.
Pinpoints of insight, lightening the gloom,
Appear and disappear

Like little galaxies;
Dark matter offered fleetingly to sight.
And all my thoughts are little more than these,
I bless the breath that lifts them to the light,
These moving mysteries.

And each breath after prayer
Is somehow shared, is somehow more than mine,
Making my little room an everywhere,
Its ordinary clutter seems to shine
Like starlight after prayer.

36

At Lee Abbey

I am writing this from Lee Abbey, set in its little hidden valley on the north coast of Devon, where the wonderful, wild and twisted oak woods slope down steep combes to the sea. This is my first visit to this astonishingly beautiful place, and Maggie and I had had a trying journey, ranging from gridlock on the M25 to wrong turns taken on to perilous single-track cliff-edge roads; so we were a little frazzled on the evening we arrived.

But what a transformation ensued! We stepped out from the house on to the terrace that first evening, just in time to see the sun going down in all its glory over the sea, and the sea itself throwing back a dazzling glitter that seemed almost brighter than the sun it reflected: a coruscating pattern in shimmering points of light, as though someone had casually spilled a tray of diamonds into a spotlight.

And then, as the sun found a bank of thin low-lying cloud, and brilliance was made bearable, everything turned to red and coppery gold and our eyes were drawn from the sea to the sky. By that time, the M25 was a world away.

I had come there to lead a series of reflections on the seven great 'I AM' sayings in St John's Gospel, drawing on the sonnet sequence that I wrote in response to those sayings; and over the course of the next few days I felt that one of those poems in particular was somehow being enacted, being transferred from the flat page to the air, the light, the landscape and the people gathered there: it was my sonnet 'I Am the Light of the World', which opens:

I see your world in light that shines behind me,
Lit by a sun whose rays I cannot see,

The smallest gleam of light still seems to find me
Or find the child who's hiding deep inside me.

The quality of the light in this part of the world is extra-ordinary, and it seemed as if the poem was simply unfolding before my tired eyes:

I see your light reflected in the water,
Or kindled suddenly in someone's eyes,
It shimmers through translucent leaves in summer,
Or spills from silver veins in leaden skies …

From that first glimpse of light reflected off the sea, to the light glinting on the rushing and tumbling waters of the Lynn as we followed it upstream, to the light of recognition and the light of discovery in people's eyes as we read John's Gospel together, to the light coming down through the canopy of leaves on our woodland walks, it was as though my list of glimpses was given back to me as a gift.

My poem continues:

It gathers in the candles at our vespers
It concentrates in tiny drops of dew,
At times it sings for joy, at times it whispers,
But all the time it calls me back to you.

And once again the images, one by one, came true: from the candles at compline to the dew on the early-morning grass; and in and through all these things, the sense of beckoning, yearning, calling, deepening still.

Climbing up from the cove, up beside the little stream of the Lee as it tumbles down to the sea, I recalled that poem's concluding couplet with renewed conviction:

I follow you upstream through this dark night
My saviour, source and spring, my life and light.

37

A Pint in the Royal Oak

I was sitting in the Royal Oak in Keswick the other day, enjoying a very fine pint of Thwaites Original and reflecting on what a blessing these old inns are. A packhorse inn in the days of Elizabeth I, and a coaching inn in the eighteenth century, this old place has been serving thirsty travellers continuously these past 400 years.

It's easy to take such continuity for granted, but in times of change and consternation, times of confusion and uncertainty such as our own, these unperturbed continuities come to mean something more: they become signs of survival and hope.

And not for the first time. As I sipped my pint I recollected a passage from a book celebrating English inns, published in 1943, in the darkest days of the Second World War. The war, of course, is never mentioned, but the book was part of a series, *Britain in Pictures*, which quietly celebrated and cherished the distinctive things that we were defending and might once have taken for granted. The sentence I recollected was this: 'The old inn is no antiquarian exhibit, no frozen relic of the past. It lives in one long continuous present.'

I love that idea of a 'long continuous present'. There had been no attempt to antiquify (if I may be permitted that word) the interior of the Royal Oak, no artfully exposed beams or battered pewter to give it a false patina of age. The furniture was comfortable and modern, the music contemporary, but that made it all the more authentically the thing it was.

For it wore no affected mustiness when Wordsworth and Coleridge came here house-hunting. And when Shelley looked in, on his way to try and track down Coleridge, it was the same plain and unpretentious hostelry that it is now. Shelley found comfortable accommodation and so did Walter Scott – indeed, he was comfortable enough to settle in for a bit and write a good portion of *The Bridal of Triermain* while he was here.

By the time Tennyson looked in for a pint, with a great deal of 'Morte d'Arthur' in his mind, which he would write out at nearby Mirehouse, the inn was on an unofficial itinerary, a sort of poetic grapevine, which also drew Robert Louis Stevenson here – and explains, I suppose, why I too was nursing my pint in this particular hostelry.

But that old book was right: this succession of poets who might all have once been sitting at my table, supping similar ale, were not 'frozen relics' but vigorously and fruitfully present to me. Their works are all in print and very much present in my mind, the stories of their lives still stir and inspire me, and each of these visitors saw the glory of the lakes and hills more distinctly because of the poetry of their predecessors, as I see and savour it all the more clearly now because of them.

But I'm glad I'll still be here on Sunday. For if a 400-year-old inn 'lives in one long continuous present', what shall we say of a parish church? For there, an even longer 'continuous present' is not merely a matter of memory and succession. There, the long continuity of unbroken worship, through the changes and chances of history, is lifted week by week into God's transfiguring presence. There, the throng of those who worshipped in the past are no mere memory but a living presence, singing the Sanctus with us in the communion of the saints.

38

The Cataract of Lodore

While on holiday in the Lakes, Maggie and I made our way to the Lodore Falls. We could hear the rushing sound of the water tumbling over rocks, falling and cascading into pools, sweeping round or splashing over every impediment, long before the path brought us round to a clear view of the steep and richly wooded chasm over which the water plunges, and is divided into many channels and cascades by the tumbled rocks in the valley, till it reunites and finds its way, at last, into Derwent Water.

There are taller falls in the Lake District and more spectacular falls in many parts of the world, but there is something deeply attractive, especially on a hot July day, about the way the falls at Lodore seem at once to rush and to loiter. They present a picture of mad, dashing, foaming activity, a constant change and movement of matter and, at the same time, they offer a singleness, almost a stillness, a steadiness; for even as the torrents of water rush past, indeed *because* they are rushing past, the waterfall is sublimely, simply and steadily being itself, remaining constant through change, still there, just as it was when Wordsworth, Coleridge and Southey stood where Maggie and I stood, to gaze on it.

It was after his brother-in-law, Coleridge, had left the household that Southey composed the famous and playful lines of 'The Cataract at Lodore' for his children. 'Tell me in rhyme how the water comes down', his little boy had asked him, and rather like the waterfall itself, Southey let rip: it comes down, he said:

... gathering and feathering,
And whitening and brightening,
And quivering and shivering,
And hurrying and scurrying,
And thundering and floundering;
Dividing and gliding and sliding ...

And so on and on, for many more lines of multiple rhymes, until the poem ends:

And so never ending, but always descending,
Sounds and motions for ever and ever are blending
All at once and all o'er, with a mighty uproar, –
And this way the water comes down at Lodore.

Southey's children loved it and ran around the garden later, reciting it madly and I too enjoyed recalling fragments of it as Maggie and I stood there absorbing the whole scene.

It was good to be there, away on holiday, unreachable, free from all interruption, and to contemplate the cataract. But even as I contemplated, I saw that what made this water-fall so beautiful was, in fact, a series of interruptions and diversions.

Water seeks the shortest course to the lowest point; so from the river's point of view, as it were, if it could speak it would be saying: 'Oh, no, I'm just trying to get down into the lake, and one damn rock after another is getting in my way', not knowing that those interruptions and impediments are its very glory; that, like poetry itself, it, as Shakespeare says, 'like the current, flies Each bound it chafes'.

Then I saw that the same was true of my own interrup-tions and diversions. As a chaplain it is my business to be interrupted, to lay down my current task and respond freely and fully to that knock on the door. I also realized that some of the best things in my literary life have happened as a result of unexpected interruptions, and that really, like this waterfall, I should exalt in them.

Mind you, it took a good holiday, free of all interruption, for me to arrive at that insight and accept it.

39

Stargazing with the Poets

Perhaps it was our recent sojourn in Keswick that put me again in mind of Coleridge; for I remembered a phrase of his just as the stars were coming out on a still evening and I was straining, against the loom of our own light pollution, to see them. I was remembering how in 'Frost At Midnight' Coleridge remembered that, at his school in London, the stars were the one thing unsmudged by the dirt of the city, the one living link with the memories of his childhood and the beauties of nature:

> For I was reared
> In the great city, pent 'mid cloisters dim,
> And saw nought lovely but the sky and stars.

Now, of course, the 'cloisters' of the city are not dim but dazzling, and you must go deep into the countryside if you want to see the stars in their proper splendour. Indeed, Coleridge himself, in a letter to a friend, remembered the brilliance of the stars in the deep Devon countryside:

> I remember that at eight years old, I walked with [my father] one winter evening from a farmer's house a mile from Ottery, and he told me the names of the stars, and how Jupiter was 1,000 times larger than our world, and that the other twinkling stars were suns, that had worlds rolling round them, and when I came home, he showed me how they rolled round.

Astronomy lessons in the vicarage with his father increased Coleridge's wonder at the 'heavens which declared the glory of the Lord', but we have even more than that: wonderful programmes on astronomy, the stars and the planets (more since the recent Moon anniversary); and, best of all, the astonishing images brought back to us from the curved and polished mirror of the Hubble Space Telescope, orbiting 'Above the smoke and stir of this dim spot Which men call earth', as Milton would have put it.

Although Coleridge had not the advantage of a polished telescope lens, the lens of his mind was polished by poetry itself: from the Psalmist to Dante and Shakespeare, for all of whom the stars were a numinous revelation, and the 'floor of heaven' was 'thick inlaid with patines of bright gold' singing a music we cannot hear.

And so I strained the other evening to see the stars myself, and make out, however faintly, through the loom of the village lights, the pale trace of the Milky Way, that gracious path through the heavens.

For it was another poet who called me to see and contemplate the Milky Way: George Herbert, who called prayer itself 'The Milky Way'. He must have seen it clearly on the nights he walked back, in that pre-industrial darkness, from Salisbury to Bemerton. From my own small village of Linton, I too gazed up; for I was trying to make a sonnet to tease out what Herbert might have meant. It came out like this:

The Milky Way

It's always there, but when our lights are low,
Or altogether out, we see it shine;
Only when things are darkest here below
Do we discern its soft pearlescent sheen,
Gracefully traced across the midnight sky,
In whose light Herbert saw the path of prayer.
Though pale and milky to the naked eye,

The view from Hubble, far above the air,
Shows us a star-field rich with many colours
'Patines of bright gold' and blue and red,
Abundance of a hundred billion stars
Whose centre lies in Sagittarius,
Darting their glory, like the myriad
Of saints and angels who all pray for us.

40

Spell

There is something magical about the act of writing itself: a summoning power inherent in the very letters of the alphabet and in the mysterious way the words they spell can summon up images – images that bring with them whole worlds.

Every act of writing evokes the hidden correspondences between Word and World: a magic witnessed by the way a word such as 'spell' means both to spell a word and to make magic, the way 'chant' is embedded in 'enchantment', the way even the dry word 'grammar' turns out to be cognate with 'glamour' in its oldest magical sense.

There has been, for me, a further kind of magic. I have been reading my poetry this summer to audiences as far afield as Vancouver, between the mountains and the sea, and Ontario, among the lakes and rivers there; and now I am in the dry plains of Indiana. All these poems started as the invocation of a few words in my little writing hut at the bottom of our garden, and yet in one sense these words have had the power to lift me on silver wings and fly me halfway across the world, to show me new sights and make me new friends. I admit that certain trains, taxis and planes were also involved in the process, but without the invocation of the poetry, nothing would have happened.

But there is, as C. S. Lewis would say, a deeper magic still. If all language is a kind of spell, it is a 'good spell' (or 'gospel' as we later shortened that term). Our faith points to a single source, in the Word, the Logos of God, for both the mystery of language and the mystery of being itself. Christ is the Word within all words, the Word behind all worlds.

Certainly many Christian writers have reflected on the

parallels between the Genesis narrative in which God says 'Let there be …' and each thing he summons springs into being; and the way the uttering of words, the combination and recombination of a finite set of letters, can call into being the imaginary worlds, the 'sub-creations', as Tolkien calls them, that God in his love has empowered us to create. It seems that being made as 'makers' (the old word for poets) is one of the ways we are all made in God's image.

Some years ago a re-reading of Tolkien's wonderful essay 'On Fairy-Stories' prompted me to celebrate the God-given power and mystery of language, the magic of naming and the summoning powers entrusted to us in the 26 letters of our alphabet, in a sonnet I simply called 'Spell':

> Summon the summoners, the twenty-six
> Enchanters. Spelling silence into sound,
> They bind and loose, they find and are not found.
> Re-call the river-tongues from Alph to Styx,
> Summon the summoners, the shaping shapes
> The grounds of sound, the generative *gramma*
> Signs of the Mystery, inscribed arcana
> Runes from the root-tree written in the deeps,
> Leaves from the tale-tree lifted, swift and free,
> Shining, re-combining in their dance
> The genesis of every utterance,
> Pattering the pattern of the tree.
> Summon the summoners, and let them sing.
> The summoners will summon Everything.

41

Orientation

One evening I found myself gazing westward towards a particularly beautiful sunset and half-remembering some lines from John Donne's 'Good Friday, 1613. Riding Westward':

> Hence is't, that I am carryed towards the West
> This day, when my Soules forme bends toward the East.
> There I should see a Sunne, by rising set,
> And by that setting endlesse day beget.

Even as Donne indulges himself in his customary love of paradox, he teases out something essential about what you might call our spiritual 'orientation': we are driven by time towards the west but drawn by God towards the east. In the outward and visible world, Donne, constrained by business, is riding westward – a direction that symbolizes the journey of all our bodies towards sunset, decline and death, westering away from the eastward moment of our morning and birth.

While Donne feels outwardly constrained to journey west, in heart and soul he wants to turn east, to turn and face towards Jerusalem, where the great drama of death and resurrection takes place.

Indeed, this spiritual orientation is outwardly expressed in the physical orientation of church buildings. Chronologically, we all face west: journeying from the morning of childhood, through the noon of our vigour and strength, towards the sunset of our waning years, where we will be lucky to escape the final cliché of a retirement home called Sunset View.

But spiritually, the reverse is the case. Our churches face east, and the font that we might associate so much with birth and babyhood is, in fact, by the west door, because it is there, even as we enter the church, that we deal with our dying. We are baptized into that sunset and declination, made one with Christ in his death, so that we might also be one with him in his resurrection, We get death over with at the outset.

Thereafter we grow younger: we move eastward towards that rising and beginning, that eternal sabbath, the first day of the week, which is our sunrise and resurrection. As St Paul so pithily put it, 'Though our outer nature is wasting away, our inner nature is being renewed every day'. C. S. Lewis also expressed this perfectly in mythopoeic form in the best of his Narnia books, *The Voyage of the Dawn Treader*, where he takes the pagan classical idea of the magical journey to the blessed isles – which, in Homer and Vergil, and in the voyages of Brendan, are all in the west – and reorients it, so we sail eastward towards sunrise.

All these and other thoughts were swirling in my mind as I gazed towards that sunset and began to compose this sonnet:

Westward

We're looking west to where our setting sun,
Already out of sight, looks back at us, to fling
His dying splendour to these clouds. They burn
With borrowed gold and crimson, not their own,
Like strips of silk torn from his royal robe,
These flags of hope left by our solar king,
Who sinks for us below the dark horizon
That he might yet encompass all this globe.
He leaves us with the promise of his rising
For all we face the west of his decline,

Already somewhere else are voices praising,
As on the east they glimpse a kindled line.
His setting is a herald of the morn,
We watch the sunset, but we tread the dawn.

42

Village Cricket

I was taking my greyhounds George and Zara out for their Saturday afternoon walk when we happened upon a cricket match on Linton village green; so, naturally, we paused to enjoy watching a few overs. Well *I* enjoyed it. George and Zara were a little puzzled by the delay in their perambulations, but I pause often enough on their behalf, so I felt they could return the favour.

There is something very satisfying about village cricket; for there you see a great sport returning to its humble origins. To witness a game in which there are more players than spectators is to be reminded of what play itself is: a thing done delightfully for its own sake, with no thought of pleasing crowds, selling tickets or, heaven forbid, promoting products.

Both teams were in whites (more or less) and moving gracefully against the rich green of the ground. The fine run and beautifully executed action of the bowler, the occasional flurry of running between the wickets or the swift darting of fielders after the ball, all were framed and punctuated by the slower ritual of changed places for the whole fielding team at the end of each over.

I watched the bowler hastening to her work, probing the batsman's defences, varying pace and pitch; and the batsman, treating the best balls with a respectful forward defensive and driving the loose ones to the boundary with a satisfying thwack, noted by the scorers, as a small boy ran excitedly to change the worn old number boards and give the running total. Reflecting on my pleasure in the whole scene, I realized that it was not simply the pleasure of an isolated moment but something richer and more cumulative: an amalgam of memory and attention.

My pleasure in the game and my appreciation of each player reaches down into the layers of memory as well as out to the game at hand: memories of my own time at the crease and as a bowler, in clergy cricket games for the diocese, and earlier still into my school days, idling in the outfield and wondering whether the ball would ever come my way, and my (very brief) moments of concentration and nerves at the crease (if it ever came down to needing the number ten batsman), my brief spells at bowling, trying to remember what my father had taught me, as a much younger boy, about the mysteries of spin. All these layers of memory and affection are somehow brought into play even in the spectacle of other people at play.

C. S. Lewis says somewhere that all our present experiences are enriched or 'thickened' by memory. He gives the example of the pleasure of breakfast. When enjoying bacon and eggs, he says, he may be eating only one rasher of bacon, but the experience and anticipation he brings to it are 'more than fifty rashers thick'.

That's a good way to put it, and as I wandered on beyond the green and towards the church, I reflected that the same is true of our experience there, where, as with cricket, we enjoy a series of familiar, repeated, ritual movements and gestures whose significance builds and thickens through many layers over time. And yet we are also vividly present and alert to the moment at hand.

Perhaps, I thought, as we idled past the church, we ought to see the opening and closing of each service as a series of 'overs' in a long and beautiful game, at whose end the hospitality of our host's pavilion awaits us.

43

Caffeaum, Carmen

Warming my hands around a mug of good strong coffee, I was musing on the great days of the coffee-house: on those gatherings of wits and scholars, warming their hands too around their coffee cups, exchanging news, making the stimulus of caffeine such a spur to ingenuity, initiative and conversation that from the coffee-houses sprang the learned societies, the political parties and, of particular interest to me, the art of the familiar essay.

It was Addison and Steele who founded and, to some degree, perfected that art in *The Spectator*, whose 'copy' was given from Will's or White's or The Turk's Head – whichever coffee-house had a reputation for conversation pertinent to that subject. Then Johnson took up the art in *The Rambler*, in concise, polished, lapidary prose, until, later still, Lamb and Hazlitt and Leigh Hunt breathed into it the new life and warmth of the romantic age. But the familiar essay began in the geniality of coffee and conversation, and often ended, on publication, being read aloud in coffee-houses as a further stimulus to more coffee and conversation.

Indeed, Hunt so longed to have witnessed the great days of the London coffee-houses that he wrote a little fantasy in which, while browsing in the back of a second-hand book shop, he finds a dusty old door that opens magically on to an eighteenth-century coffee-house.

I have never yet found that dusty door but I have found something almost as good. I have in my hands a little book, newly printed from Arc Publications, that contains the original text and a charming new verse translation of *Caffaeum, Carmen* ('Coffee, a Poem'): an encomium on coffee composed in Latin 300 years ago by l'Abbé Guillaume Massieu, a Jesuit priest turned teacher and, like most teachers, a serious coffee-drinker. His poem was just the kind of thing to recite at your local coffee-house, where the other learned coffee-drinkers would enjoy its elegance, wit and classically perfect Latin metre. Perhaps I should try it at my local Starbucks. Or perhaps not.

There are not many people who can translate neoclassical Latin verse, and of those there must be only a handful who can translate it into English heroic couplets in the style of Dryden; but John Gilmore, a lecturer in English at Warwick University, has done just that, and with great aplomb. Here's a fine passage that certainly sums up the effect on me of my first morning cup:

And sad cares Coffee chases from our hearts;
Joy to our minds its gentle strength imparts.
One have I seen, who ere the nectar sweet
He tasted, silent entered with slow feet,
And look severe, and brow with wrinkles bound.
Yet he, soon as the beverage sweet he'd down'd
And from his knitted brow fled every cloud,
With witty sayings straightway pleased the crowd.

The poem even has a passage that seems to depict a caffeinated student with an essay crisis, pulling an all-nighter. For coffee, the poet says:

Sleep from the eyes, sloth from the heart wilt drive.
These then themselves should wet with this sweet dew
Who must an end to endless tasks contrive,
Or tireless thumb their books the long night through.

I must say it doesn't surprise me that the original author of this coffee encomium was a cleric, and by no means the first or last priest to thank God for coffee.

44

A Parish Outing

There is something repellent about those slick, chic, photo-shopped holiday brochures that sometimes drop through one's letter box. Glossy photos show cloudless skies and golden beaches, which the young couple in the picture seem to have entirely to themselves as they pose, scantily clad and impossibly shaped, on luxurious sunbeds under a silken parasol, their flawless skin glistening in the Caribbean sun.

Even those pages of the brochure that reluctantly admit the existence of children admit only those who smile ecstatically from the splash pool or gaze up at their handsome and beneficent parents in awed and grateful admiration. There are no old people to be seen anywhere.

Dropping the brochures into the recycling bin, I long for some bracing antidote. And, happily, I have just been provided with one: the Linton parish outing to Great Yarmouth. Now that's a proper holiday event, a glorious world away from the brochures' corrosive fantasy: a glad celebration of the world as it actually is.

We board our coach outside the Dog and Duck, and as elderly ladies are helped aboard by the young and settle to their knitting, as a gaggle of grandchildren climb on with picnic baskets and swimming costumes, and as hard-working members of the PCC all clamber aboard looking at last relaxed and cheerful, I reckon, with some satisfaction, that we have three, perhaps four, generations: people from all walks of life, people of all shapes and sizes, all happily on board together and ready for the off.

We sweep out of the village and along the A11, flickering through Thetford forest, out into the wide flat lands of Norfolk, through the Broads, where one glimpses the windmills on either side and the strange sight of tall white sails apparently faring through open fields, sweep over the bridge at Acle and come at last to a halt on the long promenade at Great Yarmouth. From there we set off in groups, or ones and twos, to explore at our own leisure and find our own pleasures, but each clutching our copy of 'The Great Yarmouth Quiz', set by the events committee: 'Which saint is the Anglican church named after? How many of Great Yarmouth's town-wall towers are still standing?'

Remarkably, Great Yarmouth still has 11 of its medieval towers; but more remarkably, it still has most of the simple, old-fashioned pleasures of the traditional seaside holiday: the pier on which you sit in the brisk breeze eating your fish and chips, or lean out to see the donkeys trotting patiently across the sand bearing delighted children; the piratically themed 'adventure golf' course, set up as a series of ships' poops and treasure islands, where pirate figures with cutlasses between their teeth loom over you as you practise your putting skills; and, of course, best and simplest of all, the beach itself.

I walked out over the sands, just to feel that I had at least touched the sea, and observed the family groups, the buckets and spades and sandcastles, the children running with half-melted ice-creams already covered in sand, and the old couples on deckchairs already covered in newspapers.

'Still going on, all of it, still going on!' as Larkin says in 'To the Sea', a poem that celebrates 'The miniature gaiety of seasides'. Like Larkin, I was glad to know that it was all still happening as it should.

45

The Eye of the Beholder

A fine crisp morning, a little cooler than usual, and a slight scattering of leaves on the path, both seem to say, 'It's September now; the long leisure of summer is gone. Look! The Granta hurries a little faster on her journey into Cambridge, the apples are round and full enough to leave the tree. You too should quicken your step, put aside your summer meanderings, pick up some motion, excitement and purpose from these first swift rushes of the west wind, the "breath of autumn's being", and be stirring about your business, getting on with your life.'

It's strange how meaning seems to flow back and forth between ourselves and the scenes we observe, how the internal weather seems to seep into the outer and the outer into the inner. Do these stirrings and renewal of purpose in my mind and heart come out from me to clothe and interpret all I see? Or do the stirrings and changes in nature herself breathe and speak into me, to change my mind and heart?

Coleridge certainly experienced this exchange in both directions, and reflected deeply on it. In 'Frost at Midnight' he invites us to recognize the glories of nature around us as

The lovely shapes and sounds intelligible,
Of that eternal language, which thy God
Utters ...

But later, in his poem 'Dejection: An ode', he experienced it the other way round:

O Lady! we receive but what we give,
And in our life alone does Nature live …
Ah! from the soul itself must issue forth
A light, a glory, a fair luminous cloud …

But either way there is an exchange of meaning, a kind of enlightenment, some sense in which what's 'out there' tells us a little more about what's 'in here', articulates what's unspoken, makes visible what's invisible. And at the same time, all that is in here – all the memory and experience we carry – enables us to see the world out there as so much more than a mere agglomeration of physical stuff, rather as something alive with truth and mystery.

I've recently been reading a new collection, *Eye of the Beholder*, by the American poet Luci Shaw. It contains a wonderful poem called 'Bird Psalm,' in which she reflects with great clarity and precision on both sides of this experience. The poem starts with the sound of birdsong just before dawn:

Early light, before
sun, and I hear an unknown bird
singing his morning syllables –
pitiful, pitiful, pitiful – in a voice
too plaintive to be believed.

She goes on to describe birds as 'music with feathers' but confesses that, although she senses meaning, she may not have heard deeply enough to understand it:

… We pick up clues
but translation depends on our
willingness to hear, to listen.

And then, in the final verse, she opens herself, and her reader, to a new possibility, a new interpretation of the experience, in which she sets aside her own preoccupations and hears the bird-psalm differently:

Maybe
I've let last night's bad dream
misinterpret his message.
Maybe he's telling me this new day is
beautiful, beautiful, beautiful.

46

Ode 'To Autumn'

I write this on a fine September evening, conscious that it is 200 years to the very day that Keats spent a golden afternoon composing his 'To Autumn', the last of the great odes, which he completed in that *annus mirabilis* of 1819. He mentions this astonishing achievement laconically, in an almost offhand manner, in a letter to his friend Reynolds:

> How fine the air. A temperate sharpness about it … chaste weather – Dian skies – I never liked stubble fields so much as now – Aye better than the chilly green of Spring. Some-how, the stubble-plain looks warm – in the same way that some pictures look warm – this struck me so much on my Sunday's walk that I composed upon it.

And what a composition! Never can an idle Sunday after-noon have proved so fruitful, and there is indeed a 'mellow fruitfulness' about the whole poem, loaded and blessed as it is with images of ripe fruit: 'the vines that round the thatch eves run', 'the moss'd cottage trees' bending with their load of apples, the swelling gourds, the plumped hazel shells, and the bees so busy amid the late flowers that the honey in their 'clammy cells' is 'o'er brimmed' with the last of the summer.

For many years I read this ode as a straightforward hymn of praise to peace and plenty, relishing the figure of Autumn herself 'sitting careless on a granary floor', her hair 'soft-lifted by the winnowing wind', 'Or by a cyder-press, with patient look', watching 'the last oozings hours by hours'.

But more recently I have begun to read the poem in another context. Nicholas Roe's work on Keats reminds us that 1819 was the year of the Peterloo Massacre: a year of great unrest in the countryside, of bread riots and a wide sense of division and injustice in England. Roe shows that Keats was well aware of this and that the essay on the month of September by his friend the political campaigner Leigh Hunt contained not only many of the peaceful and bucolic images that Keats drew on in his ode but also a 'lesson on justice', a reminder that the other image of the season is the figure of Libra with her weighing scales, meting out just measure to each in their need. Indeed, Hunt quotes Spenser's verse on September, where the personified month holds:

> A paire of weights with which he did assoyle
> Both more and lesse, where it in doubt did stand,
> And equal gave to each as justice duly scanned.

Reflecting on Keats's lines 'And sometimes like a gleaner thou dost keep Steady thy laden head across the brook', Roe writes: 'a furrow is abandoned "half-reaped"; the gleaner – an archetype of poverty and exclusion – becomes a figure of steady purpose.'

Perhaps Keats's gleaner is still the figure of Ruth, whom he had imagined in his 'Nightingale' ode, standing 'in tears amidst the alien corn'.

If Keats could come back to this other golden September, 200 years after his ode, and scan his own country as he scanned his poem, he might find as much beauty and fruitfulness as he did then, but also, more urgently than ever, the need for balanced scales, the need to deal justice equally, the crying need to notice and have compassion on those who have no barns to fill but only glean what is left for them on the margins.

47

Proofreading

I have been examining the page proofs of my poetry collection *After Prayer*. It's a strange term, 'proofreading', and a strange task. A strange term because 'proof' itself has changed its meaning. Its first sense for us now is 'offering a knock-down proof', demonstrating a certainty, whereas its earlier sense was almost the opposite: testing a claim, questioning a certainty, probing a proposition. People say 'The exception proves the rule' as though it established the rule or 'proved' that the rule was correct, whereas the Latin original, *exceptio probat regulam*, really means that the exception probes, tries and tests the rule. Will the rule hold true, even in exceptional cases?

So my page proofs are not a 'proof' that the book is well printed but precisely an invitation to probe whether it is, to put it to the proof, to read with a critical, analytic eye.

It's a strange task, proofreading poetry, because one has constantly to hold oneself back from a deeper meaning, to hold one's imagination in check; for a proofreader cannot pass too quickly through the portal of a word into the garden it guards, but must linger on the lintel and check the workmanship of the words themselves: spelling, spacing, pagination, punctuation – everything except their all-important meaning. And so I proofread my poems in just the way I would not want my real readers to read them: 'stayed' entirely on the white surface of the paper. And in that sense, proofreading is, I hope, only preliminary, preparatory to the real reading that is to come.

I sometimes wonder whether the same isn't true of the ways we read those two far greater texts that God sends us: his World and his Word. Perhaps analytical science is a kind of proofreading of the text of the cosmos: checking it for consistency, deriving and applying the rules of its grammar, tabulating its patterns and frequencies but never quite passing through to its meaning. Perhaps we need a second and fuller reading of the world, in which the myriad appearances of nature, which we have analysed with our minds, are allowed, at last, to meet our imagination.

Maybe the same holds true for Scripture. It's odd to think that whichever translation we use, someone has spent hours proofreading the Bible that we hold in our hands, and that that too must have been a strange task, dwelling on the outer, resisting the invitation to the inner. Strange but necessary – as the printers of the so-called 'Adulterous Bible' of 1631 found to their cost, when it turned out that they had accidentally omitted the word 'not' from the seventh commandment, outraging the Archbishop of Canterbury, leading to a fine of £300 and, perhaps, to some confusion in the pews.

At least we are past the false sense of 'proof' in proofreading Scripture: skimming through the Scriptures for 'proof texts' to hurl without thought or question at those with whom we disagree; for when it comes to Scripture, the proofreading in that earlier sense of *probat* – probing, testing, trying – is all the other way round. It is Scripture that proofreads us, that probes and searches, 'pierces, even to the division of joint and marrow'. As the Psalmist says, in the old translation, which still carries that earlier, probing sense of prove: 'Examine me, O Lord, and prove me; try my reins and my heart'.

But after the proofreading, whichever way round it works, we can come, at last, to the poetry.

48

On Being Called a Wordsmith

Someone asked me recently whether I could tweak a paragraph they had written introducing a project we had both worked on. 'I'm sure you can fix this', they said. 'After all, you are our wordsmith.'

Well, I 'fixed' the piece as best I could and sent it back, a little improved, I hope; but afterwards I found myself reflecting on that term 'wordsmith'. In some ways it's very attractive – formed, I take it, on the analogy of blacksmith. (Or perhaps for some writers a silver- or goldsmith, and – in the case of the more cryptic poets – a locksmith.)

I like the idea that, just as the blacksmith labours in the forge and smithy, rendering the metals malleable in a furnace and beating them out with the ringing dint of hammer on anvil, so all those of us who work with words – all of us, journalists and preachers as well as poets – are wordsmiths, labouring in the smithy of our word-processors and notebooks, hammering the malleable material of language itself into a serviceable shape.

Indeed, I'm not the only wordsmith to have been attracted to the smithying metaphor. It is explored with great subtlety and skill in Seamus Heaney's famous early poem 'The Forge'. From its celebrated opening line, 'All I know is a door into the dark', it goes on to describe the forge and smithy, to hear 'the hammered anvil's short-pitched ring' and to see 'The unpredictable fantail of sparks' witness the 'hiss when a new shoe toughens in water'.

And then Heaney lifts us from these vivid particulars and begins to use words that suggest a deeper mystery of creation is at work here, as the anvil 'somewhere in the centre' becomes 'an altar / Where he expends himself in shape and music'. By this point in the poem we realize that the 'shape and music' evoked here includes the art of poetry, and at a deeper level suggests that the one who forges the world for us also 'expends himself' for us and is to be met at an altar.

So the image of the blacksmith behind the term 'word-smith' has a good pedigree. And yet, attractive as it is, there is something in me that hesitates to use it. I think what troubles me is the suggestion that, like the blacksmith hammering the horse's shoe, the writer (or preacher) knows in advance the exact shape that their work needs to take and can therefore hammer it into place with assurance, force and mastery.

That may be true for some writers but I find my own art to be more modest and tentative, more collaborative with its materials than dominant over them. Words, for me, are less like the hammered horseshoe and more like the horse itself: alive, frisky, strong but a little unpredictable, only to be controlled or managed as part of a long-term relationship of trust and practice built up between rider and steed.

In some ways, as a poet I aspire to be less of a blacksmith and more of a horse-whisperer: someone who can work with words, as it were, from the inside rather than hammer them from the outside. In fact my first response to good poetry, when I'm reading it, is to speak it, breathe it, whisper it into being – this gets me into trouble in libraries and bookshops; hence the whispering.

So I will leave the confident wordsmithing to others and be content instead as a word-whisperer.

49

Is it Not Enough?

I was walking George and Zara up the little path that leads from the church in Linton towards the Lady Bridge over the Granta when I came across a lovely sight: a mother watching her little girl dart eagerly here and there on the side of the path to find the conkers that had fallen so plenteously from the bordering horse chestnuts, shaken loose by the recent winds. The girl, of about five I guess, flamboyantly dressed in a purple jacket, yellow dress and sparkly gold wellington boots, was picking up and opening one conker after another as she called back joyously to her mother: 'Look, Mum! They're *everywhere!*'

But for the child's delight, neither her mother nor I might have noticed the conkers; but there they all were, bursting out of their spiky green jackets, all shiny and new. I thought of Coleridge's remark that poetry is about:

> awakening the mind's attention from the lethargy of custom, and directing it to the loveliness and the wonders of the world before us; an inexhaustible treasure, but for which in consequence of the film of familiarity and selfish solicitude we have eyes, yet see not, ears that hear not, and hearts that neither feel nor understand.

He would certainly have recognized and applauded that child's attentive wonder.

What also struck me was this little girl's delight in the sheer abundance of nature ('They're *everywhere!*'). And I remembered a poem of my own about the prodigality of autumn and the response it evokes in us. I began that poem with a question:

And is it not enough that every year
A richly laden autumn should unfold
And shimmer into being leaf by leaf,
Its scattered ochres mirrored everywhere
In hints and glints of hidden red and gold
Threaded like memory through loss and grief?

Of course, in one way it is enough and more than enough just to see and enjoy the season. Yet just as that little girl wanted not only to open the new conkers but also to call out to her mum and share her sense of discovery and abundance, just as her little shout of joy completed and crowned the pleasure of discovery, so we too, even as adults, feel a deep need to share what we see and simply to praise the praiseworthy.

In that earlier poem I went on to remember how part of my pleasure in an autumn walk is that of remembering how the poets before me have responded to the same beauty:

When scents of woodsmoke summon, in some long
And melancholy undertone, the talk
Of those old poets from whose works I drank
The heady wine of an autumnal song.

And in the end I saw that, for me too as for that little girl, the pleasure is not complete until I make some effort, as she did, to pass it on. So my poem concluded with an answer to its opening question, an answer that gestured from the leaves on the tree towards the reader who might, one day, find the poem, idly leafing through a book:

It is not yet enough. So I must try,
In my poor turn, to help you see it too,
As though these leaves could be as rich as those,

That red and gold might glimmer in your eye,
That autumn might unfold again in you,
Feeling with me what falling leaves disclose.

50

Apple Day and Evensong

This year's freshers have arrived at Girton and spent their first couple of weeks absorbing and enjoying the cornucopia of rich and sometimes strange new experiences the college and university have to offer. Most of these consist largely of free food and drink, and one of the best was Girton's Apple Day, which happily coincided with our first Sunday evensong.

For the Apple Day we brought into the dining hall samples of the rare varieties from our orchards, the fruit of so much skilful grafting and pruning. We served food with different apple sauces, washed down with apple juice or cider, and then had everyone whirling round the hall to various English country dances. I was really impressed at how willing the freshers were to fling themselves into it and have a go.

I savoured the occasion and I also savoured the apples, as much for their names as for their flavours. We had Blenheim Orange, a variety dating back to 1740, found growing against the boundary of Blenheim Park by a local cobbler, who moved it into his garden and 'thousands thronged from all parts to gaze upon its ruddy, ripening, orange burden'. We had Cox's Orange Pippin from 1825 and the stately Egremont Russet, named in 1872, as it was found on Lord Egremont's estate, although our orchard handbook adds, a little tartly, that 'its parentage is unknown'. And we had Jupiter, a jovial cross of Cox's Orange Pippin and Starking Delicious, first grafted in the swinging sixties.

And then we moved on from the orchard and the hall to the chapel. As it was the first service of the year I made it a 'guided evensong', which is to say that I introduced each part of the service with something of its history and meaning, together with the reach and the poetry of its biblical references.

I spoke a little of how the shape of the liturgy might shape and sharpen our responses and our pleasure in taking part. So I showed them how in the versicle and response 'O Lord open thou our lips. And our mouth shall show forth thy praise', we were taking on our lips the words of Psalm 51, recovering from our own confession, just as David recovered from his.

I showed how Mary's Magnificat is quite rightly the hinge between the Old and New Testament readings; for she herself fulfils the promises of the Old and gives birth to the New. And how, after we have heard that New Testament reading, it is only natural that we should all, for a moment, become old Simeon and say or sing with him, 'mine eyes have seen thy salvation'.

But it was when I told them how the service itself had been created – how Cranmer had skilfully taken the two monastic offices of vespers and compline and grafted them together into this new variety of liturgy; how he had pruned away the repetitions, let the light of translation in on the readings and allowed the whole to flourish and bear fruit for future generations – that I suddenly felt a link with our earlier Apple Day festivities.

Here too was a sturdy old English variety, adorned with early fruit (for we sang Tallis as our introit) and late beauty (our anthem was by Elgar); and here were our students, sampling in chapel, as they had done in hall, something they might otherwise never have known.

51

A Kind of Tune

My room in college is close to the chapel, which makes it easier for students to come and find me and also means that my day is laced and interwoven with scraps of music, with little snatches of tune and song, drifting out from choir rehearsals, instrumental practices and singing lessons. Indeed, when either of the organ scholars is at work I can hear something of their music, certainly the highs and lows, reaching me through two closed doors. In fact even as I write this I can hear one of them rehearsing a kind of tune.

As it happens, I have spent some time meditating on that phrase, 'a kind of tune'. It's one of the phrases used by George Herbert as an emblem for the mystery of our prayer life in his enigmatic poem 'Prayer I'. He might have meant many things by saying that prayer itself is a kind of tune. In the line before, he speaks of how prayer can 'transpose' 'the six-days world' for us: take the unsingable score of our working week and render it into a key we can manage, something within our range. So the theme of music was already in the air when he called prayer 'a kind of tune'.

Herbert was a skilled player and singer and, for him, music was always an emblem of goodness and an echo of heaven. When he missed a music practice to help a wayfarer on the road, he wrote that the memory of helping the man would itself be 'music at midnight'. John Drury recalls the story in his excellent book of that title. I wonder too whether, in calling prayer 'a kind of tune', Herbert recollected his older friend John Donne's poem in which, facing death, Donne looked forward to the moment when 'with Thy choir of saints for evermore, I shall be made Thy music'.

Herbert might also have known a great sermon of Donne's

in which he compares the creation to a stringed instrument that has gone out of tune at the Fall, and sees the coming of Christ as the sounding of a true note in humanity at last, a note we can all hear and to which we can tune ourselves:

> Angels and Men, put this instrument out of tune. God rectified all again, by putting in a new string ... the Messias, and onely by sounding that string in your eares, become we musicum carmen, true musick, true harmony, true peace to you.

I certainly had those lines of Donne as well as Herbert's poem in mind when I wrote this sonnet on the phrase 'a kind of tune' for my collection *After Prayer*:

A Kind of Tune

A kind of tune, a music everywhere
And nowhere. Love's long lovely undersong,
A trace in time, a grace-note in the air,
Borne to us from the place where we belong
On every passing breeze and in the breath
Of every creature. *All things hear and fear*,
For faintly, through our fall, we too may hear
The strong song of the Son that undoes death.

And one day we will hear it unimpaired:
The joy of all the sorrowful, the song
Of all the saints who cry 'how long',
The hidden hope of all who have despaired.
He sang it to his mother in the womb
And now it echoes from his empty tomb.

52

Dipping into Boswell

Boswell's *The Life of Samuel Johnson, LL.D.* makes wonderful bedside reading. It has the great advantage that you can open it anywhere, take up the narrative and be fed, sustained, entertained and, almost always, comforted. For it is not really a narrative at all but a series of invitations to join the company, to listen in, to feel part of that circle of stimulating talk, judicious observation, wit – in its widest and deepest sense – and long, strong, unemphatic but always hospitable Christian fellowship.

Once the initial story of his life and achievements, up to his meeting with Boswell, has been told, the rest of the book, and far the largest part, is really a series of nourishing and entertaining anecdotes: you can open the book and close it where you please without losing the thread; for there is no thread to lose. And when you do open it, almost at random, your eye is sure to fall on something like this: 'There was a pretty large circle this evening. Dr Johnson was in good humour, lively and ready to talk upon all subjects.'

And then away you go, romping through topics that, though occasionally 'dated', are often surprisingly modern in their reach and thought: Why is it that female domestics are invariably paid less than their male equivalents? Surely, says the great doctor, this offends against natural justice. Then there are little glimpses of newfangled inventions, which we know – though Boswell doesn't – will change everything:

Mr Ferguson, the self-taught philosopher, told him of a new-invented machine which went without horses: a man who sat in it turned a handle, which worked a spring that drove it forward. 'Then, Sir, (said Johnson,) what is gained is, the man has his choice whether he will move himself alone, or himself and the machine too.'

Ah, the new invention for dealing with burdens that turns out to be a new burden – if only we had the good doctor's opinion on the invention of email! And then the conversation turns to family affections. Are they innate or acquired? Then it turns, just as naturally and unaffectedly, to faith and theology, and Johnson, surprisingly, sets out the Roman Catholic doctrine of purgatory with great understanding and sympathy:

> They are of the opinion that the generality of mankind are neither so obstinately wicked as to deserve everlasting punishment, nor so good as to merit being admitted into the society of blessed spirits; and therefore that God is graciously pleased to allow of a middle state, where they may be purified ...

Sometimes I read with envy and wish that I too, at the end of a stressful or harassing day, could be admitted to that circle of leisurely and genial conversation, where real disagreements are entertained with such charity.

But then I see that Johnson attained that calm and largesse even in the midst of his own stresses and hassles. As he puts it, far better than I could, in a letter of apology to Boswell for not having written sooner: 'Sir, I have been hindered, I know not how, by a succession of petty obstructions.'

A classic sentence! I think that's how I will begin the next apologetic email I have to write, for missing a meeting or failing to keep up with my own correspondence.

53

An Excursion

The other morning, at an uncomfortably early hour, I made my way to St Pancras Station. I paid my respects to the fine statue of Betjeman, holding on to his hat, his coat blown back in an imaginary wind as he gazes up at the great ceiling that he did so much to save. Then, having touched base with Sir John, I set off on the hunt for clergy. They were not far to find, and I soon joined a great crowd of them, clustered around the departure area for Eurostar.

Perhaps 'crowd' is too poor a word for the rich collection of individuals that gathered there. Is there a better collective noun? A posse of priests? A collation of clergy? A vaguery of vicars? Whatever our collective noun, we were slowly collected together and made our way, I might almost say processed, to and through ticketing and security, and were soon settled into a couple of carriages and on our way to Merville, the little town, once Flemish and now in the Hauts-de-France, whose cloistered diocesan retreat house was hosting us for a conference of the Two Cities Area of London diocese.

I was there as a speaker and poet-in-residence; but I was also there, as the Irish would say, 'for the craic', of which there was plenty. The cities of London and Westminster have between them so many beautiful old churches, so many extraordinary, diverse, eclectic and contrasted con-gregations, churchmanships and traditions, all with diverse, eclectic and intriguing clergy to match.

Indeed, as the conference unfolded I was put in mind of Betjeman again, remembering the story of how he was once asked to give a talk on the 'C of E'. 'I've been puzzling all week,' he began, 'over what these mysterious initials stand for. My first observations led me to believe that they stood for "Comedy of Errors", but on closer examination I see that they really mean "Co-inherence of Extremes".'

While there are extremes in the flamboyance and ardour of high and low churchmanship on offer in the churches of the two cities, I was impressed at this conference by the degree of coinherence too. Coinherence, as Charles Williams asserted, involves a mutual indwelling, a recognition, in and through difference, of the sustaining presence and coherence of Christ in us, the hope of glory. There was, of course, plenty of convivial ribbing and teasing but there was also a level of mutual recognition.

I'm sure the place itself was part of that. Not just the good French food and wine on offer but also something more. As we travelled from Lille to Merville we passed the signs to the battlefields of both world wars, and in all those flat Flanders fields there were no trees more than 100 years old, no old buildings that had not been completely rebuilt from ruins. We were travelling deep into a land of death and resurrection.

In the retreat-house garden they had set the Stations of the Cross, beautifully painted. But beneath each image of the Passion, on this local *Chemin de Croix*, were black-and-white photographs, taken in 1919, of all the neighbouring churches, desolate and ruined and with scarcely one stone left standing on another. Yet from that garden you could scan the horizon and see their spires, risen again to the sky.

As we returned from the conference, each to conduct Remembrance Sunday services according to our own tradition, we had every reason to be glad of our coinherence in Christ, and to be bearers of the good news of resurrection.

54

Old and Worn

My birthday falls in November; so, naturally, I look back a little and sometimes forward, reflecting on the passage of time. This year I somehow found myself remembering a November night 20 years ago – the year we were all being asked to prepare for the millennium!

A little notice appeared in the post-office window in Fenstanton, where we lived, advertising a meeting to start a 'Fenstanton Millennium Band' to play for the festivities, planned to take place around the village clock-tower on New Year's Eve. So I blew the dust off my old guitar and showed up to see what would happen.

Arriving at the village hall I could already hear the loud wailing of electric guitars and the clatter of synthesized drums, and soon realized, once I stepped in, that all the other contenders had gone out and bought the latest shiny gear, including auto-loop pedals and drum machines, and were all trying them out at full volume.

Well, we did form a band, and in spite of my less-than-pristine guitar I found myself rocking round the clock with the others as the new millennium dawned. But on the night of that audition I went home and wrote a song about my old guitar, which became a defence of all that's old and worn. It started with a verse and chorus like this:

I was round rocking with the boys, they showed me all
   the latest toys,
They've got gizmos now that could almost play the gig.
They like to tell me money talks, they sure can make
   those boxes squawk,
They say by spending out they're bound to make it big.

121

But my guitar is old and worn, made the year that I
    was born,
You could put it down as only wood and string
But when I open up that case and blow the dust from off
    its face
And lift it up, sometimes I swear I can hear it sing …

I sang the song a few days later at a gig for my birthday, and
I still occasionally take it out at this time of year. Indeed, the
verses I wrote two decades ago about savouring the passage
of time seem more pertinent to me now than they did then:

Now as I watch my life unroll, I read the poems on
    the scroll
And I do my best to savour every line
And every year that takes its toll, is laid down deep
    within my soul
But I can draw it up again like vintage wine …

After each verse I came back to the chorus about taking my
guitar out of its case, but when it came to the final verse and
chorus I changed it around a little. Perhaps I was remembering Donne's lines about being made God's music, and
perhaps, even in this dark time of year, I wanted a little hint
of the Easter to come.

    I still sing this song in pubs, although the 'touch of grey'
in the final chorus has since become a full cascade. The song
ends like this:

Now this box of mellowed wood, sounds every bit
    as good
As the day its maker blessed it with a string
I can see it lying in the shade, remembering every note
    it's played

And waiting for the day that'll let that music ring.
So I don't mind my touch of grey, I'm not fearing for
the day
When every buried seed is bound to have its spring.
When Someone opens up my case, I know I'll see Him
face to face
And when I'm in my Maker's hands, He'll hear me sing!

55

A Winter Morning Reverie

After a 'season of mists and mellow fruitfulness', Linton has felt, at last, the first hard frosts of winter. Yet these too have their own beauty: sharp, severe but still scintillating. I walked this morning with George and Zara where the low winter sun, dazzling in the crisp dry air, lit up the last leaves still clinging to the trees, shining through them in translucent red and gold, and coruscating off of the frosted grass in the village green with an almost preternatural intensity. Other dog-walkers, approaching between me and the sun, seemed haloed and resplendent, and I had to shade my eyes to see them.

George and Zara, clad in their burgundy winter coats, were picking their way delicately and a little dubiously through the sharp blades of frozen grass, but I was enjoying the crunch of frost beneath my boots and the clouds of my frosted breath hanging in the air.

The Granta was still free-flowing though; and, lingering by one of its little falls and rivulets for the pleasure hearing the water and for the lovely patterns it makes when it streams away beneath its fall, I realized I was enjoying water simultaneously in all three of its forms: the bright ice-crystals frosting the trees, the liquid purling and falling in the stream, and the little clouds, the vapour of suspended droplets in the air that made my breath visible.

I remembered how Lao Tzu thought that the Tao, the true way as he understood it, was like water:

The highest good is like that of water. The goodness of water is that it benefits the ten thousand creatures; yet itself does not scramble, but is content with the places

124

that all men disdain. It is this that makes water so near the way.

I remembered that for St Francis too there was something in the very quality of water, seeking the lowest place, cleansing and purifying, that seemed to sing humility into the soul:

Praised be You my Lord through Sister Water,
So useful, humble, precious, and pure.

For me too, contemplating in stream and frost and cloudy breath the three lovely forms of Sister Water, there was a sense that the outward was expressing the inward. I have always thought of language itself as a stream, flowing unbidden from a hidden source, flowing in and through us, making a network of channels between us, irrigating our minds with meaning.

Now I wondered whether water's other forms might also tell me a little more about language itself. The frost around me glittered like a scattering of diamonds, and I thought of how some words, or whole phrases, can suddenly crystallize a meaning for us, illuminate it, show it in all its facets.

I thought of how a haiku or a sonnet can take a moment in the flow of language and hold it up in bright crystalline, perfectly structured form before it melts and flows away once more. And I thought too of how my frosted breath, flowing free from me, forming its own cloud-shapes, catching the light of the low sun, was like the flux of half-formed images, the 'shaping fantasies', as Shakespeare called them, that just precede speech itself: a free-floating cloud of imagination that has not yet precipitated into words.

My thoughts might have floated free a little longer, but there was a sharp tug at the leads and George and Zara soon had me back on their track through the frost, back to a warm house, a strong coffee, and more serious work.

56

An Advent Fantasy

About this time of year, amid all the stresses of the season, I find myself indulging in a recurring fantasy: I imagine the approach of December, and Advent itself, as a time of rich quietude, untrammelled leisure and mellow contemplation. I imagine low lights, quiet streets, almost deserted shops and time spent simply and inexpensively at home with one's family.

I imagine harassed parents saying to one another, as December approaches, bringing Advent with it, 'Oh, I'm so glad we've got to this time of year again! It's such a relief to know we'll have a complete break from the rush and bustle, no extra events in the school calendar, a chance for the kids to calm down a little before the big feast, and some space and time for us to be still as well.'

'Yes,' one would reply; 'and it's so nice that all the firms have agreed not to advertise anything during Advent, not to keep urging us to spend, spend, spend. And it's lovely too the way the shops spread those simple curtains over the displays they're working on, so one's eyes are not distracted or tired by constantly flashing lights.'

'Yes,' says the other, 'four wonderful weeks of calm and simplicity, and then, of course, we can really enjoy the dazzling contrast, when it all changes so suddenly and dramatically on Christmas Eve! When the curtains are drawn back and the shops reveal their beautiful displays, and all the Christmas lights are lit. Then it really is Christmas; then we decorate the tree and we can delight in the lights and the glory and the presents and parties – all of it just for those special 12 days.'

'Yes, and 12 days is just about right. I enjoy it well enough, but I'm not sure I could take much more than that.'

'You're so right; I know that, in the bad old days, when the shops were in charge, it used to go on for ages and pall on people terribly.'

'So it did. Well, enjoy your quiet Advent this December.'

It is usually at about this point in the fantasy that my reverie is interrupted by some loud commercial announcement, some tinny Christmas music in a shop, blared out before Advent has even begun, and I'm back to reality.

But maybe things are changing. I sense a reaction coming. I sense a yearning for Advent again, for the fast before the feast. And I know that growing numbers of people have found ways of setting time aside to prepare for his coming, to yearn again for his light, to remember who he is and what he brings.

I once reflected that I'd like CAMRA, the Campaign for Real Ale, to be CAMRE, a Campaign for Real Evangelism. But it now occurs to me that if CAMRA was a Campaign for Real Advent as well as for real ale, then one might enjoy another happy parallel. One might start a Christmas brew fermenting on the First Sunday of Advent, bubbling away in a dark cupboard and quietly strengthening, and at the same time one might begin a little spiritual ferment: a deepening of faith, a sweetening of hope, a strengthening of love, all kept out of sight, all working from within until, when Christmas itself arrived, the ale and the alleluias would both be ready to be uncorked and shared together.

57

Whitby

Perhaps it's my Scots and Yorkshire ancestry, but I am always exhilarated by travelling north, and feel a sense of vigour, of something brave and bracing, when I come into Yorkshire, especially when the road lifts me up over the moors and on towards the sea.

Such was the road that has brought me for a few days to Whitby, where I am giving a poetry retreat at St Hilda's Priory for the Sisters there, the Order of the Holy Paraclete. Their new convent buildings, in the grounds of their old castle-priory, overlook the curved bay and snug harbour of Whitby, and you gaze from their grounds over the town itself and out to the other headland, where the medieval abbey stands in all its ruined splendour.

So the town is flanked and protected, as it were, by these two religious houses: the old abbey, with its memories of Hilda, the great saint of the past, and the new one, where Hilda's faith is still practised and her name and wisdom are still venerated. Of course, Hilda's monastery, of Streoneshalh, as both the place and the abbey were then called, long predates the Benedictine abbey whose ruins still stand; but the figure of Abbess Hilda herself towers above these wrecks of time and seems more relevant and timely to us than ever.

Hilda is famous for having presided over the Synod of Whitby in 664, and for having striven to bring peace and a single Church out of the two strands of Roman and Celtic Christianity. But to my mind it's another story that Bede tells of her that resonates more strongly and makes me venerate this place even more deeply, and that is the story of Caedmon, the earliest English poet whose name we know

– perhaps the first Christian poet in England, and thus the archetype of my own vocation.

According to Bede, Caedmon was a lay Brother who cared for the animals at the monastery here. When there was feasting and the harp was passed along for songs and poetry, Caedmon would slip out to the byre, on the pretext of tending to the animals; for he didn't reckon himself a poet. But once, as he dozed there, an angel came to him in a dream and told him to sing 'The beginning of created things'. Caedmon refused at first, then suddenly found that he could do it, and composed a poem praising the 'fashioner of Heaven's high fabric'.

Bede goes on to tell how the Abbess heard both the story and the poem, and fostered Caedmon's talent, establishing at Whitby a school for poetry in the English tongue. Now, like Caedmon before me, I too have been summoned by the nuns of Whitby to read them my poems and reflect on our faith together.

So I happily recall a poem I once wrote honouring Hilda and Caedmon, and the space this unique place has made for poetry:

Hilda of Whitby
Called to a conflict and a clash of cultures,
Where insults flew whilst synod was in session,
You had the gift to find the gift in others,
A woman's wisdom, deftness and discretion.
You made a space and place for poetry
When outcast Caedmon, crouching in the byre,
Was called by grace into community
And local language joined the Latin choir.

Abbess we need your help, we need your wisdom,
Your strong recourse to reconciliation,

Your power tempered by God's hidden Kingdom,
Your exercise of true imagination.
Pray for our synods now, princess of peace,
That every fettered gift may find release.

58

Heaven in Ordinary

Of all the luminous and generative phrases in George Herbert's astonishing poem 'Prayer I', 'Heaven in ordinary' is both the most famous and the most suggestive. Scholarship has opened up some of the rich possibilities in that phrase that a modern reader might miss, but it remains just as suggestive, generous and generative for the 'ordinary' reader.

All of us who have read Herbert's poem and savoured this phrase can have an immediate sense of what he means: that prayer itself sometimes lifts a veil and allows us to see the ordinary and everyday transfigured for a moment – to glimpse the temporal made suddenly lucid and lucent with a touch of eternity.

The phrase always seems to summon that other famous verse of Herbert's that we sing together in church:

A man that looks on glass,
On it may stay his eye;
Or if he pleaseth, through it pass,
And then the heaven espy.

Just for a moment, the glassy surface of the world, dusty and familiar, is cleared and cleansed; something shines through and we have a brief anticipation of St Paul's great hope for us all: that although 'now we see through a glass darkly', one day 'we shall know as we are known'; one day 'we shall see face to face' and the face we shall see is the face of Love.

But scholars who have studied the many ways the word 'ordinarie' was used in Herbert's day can offer some additional insights. They point out, for example, that 'the ordinarie' was a phrase used by innkeepers. When a traveller arrived at an inn, he would be asked whether he would like a bespoke supper, brought to him upstairs in a private room, or whether he would be happy to have 'the ordinarie' with the other travellers, and sit round the fire with 'the company' in the common room. The 'ordinarie' was whatever happened to be cooking in the common pot, ladled up and served round in earthenware vessels at the common table.

If Herbert was playing on that sense of the word, then he might be suggesting that prayer enables us to glimpse and discern heaven itself in the midst of our common life together, in the shared meal, the chance encounter, the acknowledgement of our common humanity, our common pilgrimage. We don't always have to go into a private room, shut the door and pray in secret (though our Lord tells us that that is sometimes necessary).

Perhaps Herbert is even hinting that we'll glimpse the heaven in our midst only if we give up a few of our exclusive privileges and entitlements, and are happy to throw in our lot with 'ordinary' folk. That interpretation is strengthened by the fact that in his striking poem 'Christmas I', Herbert imagines himself as just such a weary traveller arriving at an inn. But it turns out that by some slip in the fabric of space and time, the poet's nearest inn, 'the next inne he could find', is the inn at Bethlehem:

> I took up in the next inne I could finde,
> There when I came, whom found I but my deare,
> My dearest Lord, expecting till the grief
> Of pleasures brought me to him, readie there
> To be all passengers most sweet relief?

And having arrived to find his Saviour unexpectedly waiting for him at the inn, he turns to address Christ himself:

O Thou, whose glorious, yet contracted light,
Wrapt in night's mantle, stole into a manger;
Since my dark soul and brutish is thy right,
To Man of all beasts be not thou a stranger.

And the link to Christmas goes, I think, even deeper. If I were to look for one phrase that sums up the whole of Christmas, that tells me the true heart and meaning of the incarnation itself, it would be 'Heaven in ordinary'. At Christmas, heaven comes down to earth, for heaven is not really a place but a person. To be in heaven is to be fully and delightedly in the presence of the living God, and to know his presence as Love. We sing that truth together in Faber's great hymn 'Immortal Love':

Alone, O Love ineffable,
Thy saving name is given;
To turn aside from thee is hell,
To walk with thee is heaven.

At Christmas, that 'Love ineffable' is ineffable no more but comes to us and takes a name, comes to be present with us, comes into the midst of the ordinary: the crowded inn, the beasts at the byre, the straw and muck of the manger. Perhaps it is because heaven was able to be 'in ordinary' at the inn that we can all occasionally glimpse heaven in the ordinariness of our own lives.

59

A Cup of Kindness

I always enjoy the seasonal bout of Burns-singing at the turn of the year, and sway to 'Auld Lang Syne' with the best of them, however dubious our harmonies or pronunciation might become as the night wears on. Though it's usually only the first verse and chorus (sometimes just the chorus) that's sung south of the border, it's a fine song in all its verses. However oblique their meaning may be to the English, their spirit (in every sense of that term) is eminently clear and always well interpreted: a spirit of camaraderie, of kindness, of holding together, a debonair defiance of the cold and dark, a spirit perfectly expressed by the spirited Mr Micawber:

> 'I may say, of myself and Copperfield, in words we have sung together before now, that
>> We twa hae run about the braes
>> And pu'd the gowans' fine
> – in a figurative point of view – on several occasions. I am not exactly aware,' said Mr. Micawber, with the old roll in his voice, and the old indescribable air of saying something genteel, 'what gowans may be, but I have no doubt that Copperfield and myself would have frequently taken a pull at them, if it had been feasible.'

But it's not the phrase about pulling the gowans (daisies) that always comes home to me, rather the oft-repeated phrase 'We'll tak a cup o' kindness yet'.

I love that phrase; for it gets to the heart of true conviviality. However large or small the 'cup' – and it's a 'pint-stoup' in Burns's second verse – and whatever the tipple may be, it is kindness itself that we exchange and quaff together.

We raise the cup and pledge our affections, and what we share in the cup is kindness: our fellow-feeling, our tenderness to one another, our compassion; for running and skirling beneath the uplifting melody of this song, like a bagpiper's drone, is a note of elegy, of melancholy, a tacit acknowledgement of all that time takes from us. 'Auld lang syne' – the vanished 'old long since', the days gone by – may seem to return as we sing, but only in memory: memories that speak of loss even as they seem for a moment to restore the past, and evoke the departed. We never sing this song without also remembering and grieving for absent friends, and then we need all the kindness we can get.

When Burns first gave this song to the world in *The Scots Musical Museum*, he claimed that 'Auld Lang Syne' was 'an old song and tune which has often thrilled thro' my soul'. But scholars now think that it was almost entirely his own composition. He was shy, perhaps, of innovating within a tradition, and perhaps secretly wished that it was traditional. If so, he has his wish now; for the song has soared above its little nest of particular authorship and flown, a free spirit, into every soul.

And Burns's poetic intuition that, whatever is in the cup 'outwardly and visibly', its real meaning is something more than malt, returns to me when I turn from the raised glass to the raised chalice. If ever there was 'a cup of kindness', it is there on the altar. There, indeed, a friend from 'auld lang syne' is truly present with us again, and the cup of his kindness overflows.

60

In Rivey Wood

In a fit of January self-improvement I have taken to climbing Rivey Hill. Linton is proud to nestle below one of the few hills in Cambridgeshire, and whereas many counties wouldn't go so far as to call it a hill at all, in the flatlands of East Anglia it seems positively Alpine, towering up to its full 367 feet and crowned with a quirky water tower that seems oddly reminiscent of a Chinese pagoda.

But the chief pleasure of Rivey Hill is not the exertion of the ascent up the ancient Icknield Way between open fields but the descent through Rivey Wood. The wood covers one part of the hill and looks just like those drawings of 'the Wild Wood' in *The Wind in the Willows* that so kindled many a childhood imagination.

There is, indeed, something magical, some kindling of imagination, every time one steps into a wood; for woods, it seems to me, never lose their rich mythical and literary associations: the greenwood tree, the forest of Arden, the wild wood, the dark forest, Lothlorien, the wood between the worlds.

Charles Williams, the poet, novelist and theologian, felt that sense of literary rootedness, of branching and interleaving, in the very idea of a woodland, and he wrote, in his remarkable book on Dante, *The Figure of Beatrice*, that 'the image of a wood' in literature has become, in all of our minds, 'a great forest where, with long leagues of changing green between them, strange episodes of high poetry have place. Thus in one part there are lovers of a midsummer night, or by day a duke and his followers … in another a poet listening to a nightingale …'

Perhaps the woodland is itself a symbol of the imagination: rooted, growing, endlessly branching out and ever changing.

If you can't step into the same river twice, then you certainly can't step into the same wood. I have walked through Rivey Wood in every season, from the first fresh, tender green when budded leaves put forth, through the carpets of blue-bells in May, to the rich, almost infinitely variegated greens of high summer, to all the ochres of autumn.

And now the wood is in its winter beauty. I step from the main track on to the little path that leads into the wood, and even in January I am in another world: last autumn's leaves lie dried and brown in rich drifts at my feet, and the trees themselves, naked now, reveal their lovely shapes at last. They throw out their branches in extravagant, twisted, impossible gestures. The elderly and infirm have tottered gracefully and half-fallen into the arms of the young, and I must stoop beneath their aged trunks where they cross the path at shoulder height.

My ascent was open, straight and narrow, but coming down through the wood, the dogs and I take twists and turns, lose and find our path, descend into little valley-folds damp with rivulets and rising springs, and re-ascend past the open-mouthed burrows of other, earthier, more ancient denizens of this wood. George and Zara can scarcely contain their excitement.

My thought also takes new turns in a wood; fresh possi-bilities for poetry suggest themselves. Indeed, I sometimes sense that if I stood still long enough a new poem might emerge from cover, fully formed, and show itself, like a shy deer. But my greyhounds haven't the patience for that.

61

Time

I love those odd corners of London where, unexpectedly, in the midst of the modern, one stumbles suddenly on some living continuity with the distant past; the long, strange, hardy persistence of deep-rooted things in the city and the realm. The Royal Foundation of St Katharine, in Limehouse, returned in the last century to its old home in the East End, is one such place, and I was glad to be there for a few days, leading a retreat on poetry and prayer.

It was founded, astonishingly, in 1147, by Queen Matilda, who called it 'my hospital next to the Tower of London' – a 'hospital' in the full medieval sense: a place of prayer with a chapel, a place of hospitality with hostel and almshouses, a place of healing, and as time went by and the trade along the Thames grew, a place of sanctuary for wanderers from many countries.

Over the mantelpiece is a sixteenth-century portrait of a former Master of St Katharine's. His weathered, wise and timeworn face gazes out at you from above a magnificent lace ruff and from beneath a ceremonial hat that looks strikingly like a child's drawing of a crown. He could be one of the Magi from a Renaissance painting, but his name was Julius Caesar! He was, in fact, the son of an Italian immigrant who had made his way up the river, and also, it would seem, up the strata and echelons of English society. St Katharine's flourished under his stewardship, and he left his ladder there for others.

I felt his benign presence in the chapel, where his pulpit has been restored and where I began the retreat with the poetry of his younger contemporary, Shakespeare. Soon we were crossing seamlessly back and forth between the centuries, reading sonnets on poetry and prayer as though the compass-rose inlaid in the chapel floor, with its centre of rose-coloured granite from St Catherine's Monastery on Mount Sinai, were magically transporting us in a time-ship, travelling, as the inscription round that compass says, 'not by navigation but by Love'.

You carry with you that sense of time-slip, of the interplay between past and present, even as you step beyond St Katharine's walls. That evening I wandered along by the pubs of Narrow Street, where The Grapes has stood these 500 years, leaning precariously out over the Thames, as Dickens said, 'like a faint-hearted diver, who has paused so long on the brink that he will never go in at all'.

And when, having walked along by Regent's Canal from Limehouse Basin to the Mile End Road, I stepped in to a little shop for coffee, my meditations on time were interrupted, or perhaps concluded, by a strange encounter. The shop seemed empty but suddenly the door opened and a man strode in, took one look at me and with a cry of recognition said: 'You're from the sixteenth century!' I was a little taken aback but he would brook no denial. 'You're from centuries ago, I know you are. You're a time traveller, but you're welcome.'

There was, it is true, more than a whiff of brandy on his breath, and perhaps it was my beard, my stick, my broad-brimmed hat or his own inward agenda that gave this gentleman of the road such certainty. But after we parted, with a chink of change, and I made my way down the darkening towpath, I began to wonder whether he might be right after all about the time travel, and whether I hadn't better be hastening back to my chapel-Tardis at St Katharine's.

62

In the Rabbit Room

I was giving a lecture in Oxford the other day and took the opportunity, as I often do, to drop into the Eagle and Child. It's a fine old seventeenth-century pub, unspoiled by 'improvement'; it still has a couple of those lovely wood-panelled 'snugs' that encourage camaraderie and close conversation – and, most famously, 'the Rabbit Room', where C. S. Lewis, J. R. R. Tolkien, Charles Williams and their friends met on Tuesday lunchtimes for the kind of sparring, cajoling but ultimately encouraging conversation that was at the heart of their informal club, the Inklings. As Lewis said of these pub sessions, in a letter to his friend Arthur Greeves: 'The fun is often so fast and furious that the company probably thinks we're talking bawdy when in fact we're very likely talking theology.'

It's a pleasure to raise a pint to their memory in that room and to imagine the free flow of their talk, to think of how the solid goodness, the conviviality and welcome that Tolkien evoked in the Prancing Pony, might owe something to this place. Indeed, life sometimes imitates art, and on one occasion, Tolkien recalled: 'I noticed a strange tall gaunt man, half in khaki, half in mufti, with a large wide awake hat and a hooked nose sitting in a corner. The others had their backs to him but I could see in his eye that he was taking an interest in the conversation.'

Moments later the stranger leaned forward and took up the thread of what was being said, and was discovered to be the poet Roy Campbell, who had come from South Africa to Oxford specifically to seek out Lewis and Tolkien. Tolkien reflected that it was just like the moment when Strider is revealed at the Prancing Pony, an episode from the unfinished *New Hobbit*, which he had only recently read to his fellow Inklings.

So as I sat in that dark little snug, nursing my pint, in the same corner, if not the same chair as that wayfaring poet, I savoured the way literary inns enhance one's appreciation of real inns and vice versa.

The other good thing about The Bird and Baby, as the Inklings called it, is that it is just a few doors down from the Oxfam bookshop, which as one would expect in Oxford, is always well stocked, and sometimes I pop in there on my way to the pub. On this occasion I picked up a nice hardback edition of Seamus Heaney's translation of *Beowulf*, a choice of which both Tolkien and Lewis would have approved. Enjoying the happy combination of beer and Beowulf, I recalled that 'Beer and Beowulf' was in fact the name Lewis gave to his Anglo-Saxon tutorials at Magdalen. How much more attractive a title than 'Linguistics 101: The Vowel Shift'!

Before I drained my pint, I recited (under my breath) a little tributary sonnet to Lewis:

From 'Beer and Beowulf' to the seven heavens,
Whose music you conduct from sphere to sphere,
You are our portal to those hidden havens
Whence we return to bless our being here.
Scribe of the Kingdom, keeper of the door
Which opens on to all we might have lost,
Ward of a word-hoard in the deep heart's core,
Telling the tale of Love from first to last.
Generous, capacious, open, free,
Your wardrobe-mind has furnished us with worlds
Through which to travel, whence we learn to see
Along the beam, and hear at last the heralds
Sounding their summons, through the stars that sing,
Whose call at sunrise brings us to our King.

63

Hunkering Down

These long weeks as January turns, interminably it seems, towards February, and February itself begins so slowly, stuck in its own mire, oppressed by its own lowering clouds: these weeks can be trying, especially for those of us who crave the light and are naturally, and seasonally, cast down by the darkness and drench of winter; those of us for whom there is a hidden pact between the outer and the inner weather.

John Clare, the great 'peasant poet' who wrote with such exact and compassionate observation of the fields and seasons of his native Northamptonshire, felt these things deeply too. He noted that in February it's not so much the continuation of January's winteriness as the little thaws, the patches and snatches of warmth, the apparent promises of spring, summoning you out, only to turn bitter again and freeze you, that are the most trying.

The poem for February in his *The Shepherd's Calendar* is filled with wonderful observations of nature. The Shepherd sees the sheep waking up to the hope of spring:

> The flocks as from a prison broke
> Shake their wet fleeces in the sun
> While following fast a misty smoke
> Reeks from the moist grass as they run

And even his dog seems caught up in the promise of warmth and light:

> Nor more behind his masters heels
> The dog creeps on his winter pace
> But cocks his tail, and oer the fields
> Runs many a wild and random chase

My dogs do much the same in the sun-thaw but, of course, there is a catch: it is still only February, and our hopes have surged a little too soon. So Clare, in a single stanza, sighs away his glimpse of spring:

Thus Nature of the spring will dream
While south winds thaw but soon again
Frost breaths upon the stiffening stream
And numbs it into ice …

Nevertheless, for all its delays the spring always comes and, in the meantime, it's a case of hanging on through gritted teeth, hunkering down – 'Wintering out The back end of a bad year', in Seamus Heaney's phrase.

When it comes to courage and endurance, I find that poetry helps: just knowing that so many of the poets I admire have been through this too and given it voice makes me feel companioned and encouraged, and even prompts me to have a go myself at voicing both the bleakness and the genuine promise of release, as I did in this sonnet:

Because We Hunkered Down

These bleak and freezing seasons may mean grace
When they are memory. In time to come
When we speak truth, then they will have their place,
Telling the story of our journey home,
Through dark December and stark January
With all its disappointments, through the murk
And dreariness of frozen February,
When even breathing seemed unwelcome work.

Because through all of these we held together,
Because we shunned the impulse to let go,

Because we hunkered down through our dark weather,
And trusted to the soil beneath the snow,
Slowly, slowly, turning a cold key,
Spring will unlock our hearts and set us free.

64

A Message from Wuhan

Back in January, when coronavirus seemed only a distant prospect, a blur on the edge of our screens, I received an unexpected message from Wuhan. A woman there, self-isolating within that greater isolation, because she had symptoms, had taken comfort in one of my sonnets and wanted to let me know. As I read her message on social media, the world seemed suddenly smaller, the distant prospects close. I asked which poem it was and was amazed to learn it was my sonnet on Julian of Norwich! I was sur-prised at first but then it all made sense. My correspondent, a Christian teaching in the International School in Wuhan, had suddenly found herself, willy-nilly, walled in, and even within the city walls, further enclosed in her own room, looking out through a window, receiving food through a hatch. What could she do but read and pray? And of course her thoughts turned to Julian, for Julian was a woman who had chosen, and made fruitful, just such enclosure as my correspondent was now enduring. Julian was a woman in a city many times menaced by plague, ill herself, who never-theless through and in that illness sought a new intimacy with Christ and found his wounds touching and redeeming hers. She was an anchoress who had found again her anchor-hold in God, holding strong and steady amid the tides of panic and blame that turned and shifted around her. Indeed, she swam against, and helped to turn, a tide of bad theol-ogy. In a time when illness was deemed to be a judgement from God and a sign of sin, Julian prayed to be made ill that she might come closer to Christ. In an age that considered outbreaks of infection a sign only of wrath and condemna-tion, she discerned that Christ knows and loves and holds us even and especially when we suffer, and that his meaning, his intent towards us in all things, is only love.

My reader in Wuhan, I'm glad to say, has fully recovered, but it may be that by now some of my readers here have also become accidental anchorites or anchoresses, and might also take hope and comfort in Julian, might learn afresh from her. So I hope these words, which I composed years ago in Julian's little cell in Norwich and which found their way to Wuhan, might also be useful to some of us now, wherever we might happen to be walled in.

Julian of Norwich

Show me, O anchoress, your anchor-hold
Deep in the love of God, and hold me fast,
Show me again in whose hands we are held,
Speak to me from your window in the past,
Tell me again the tale of Love's compassion
For all of us who fall on to the mire,
How he is wounded with us, how his passion
Quickens the love that haunted our desire.
Show me again the wonder of at-one-ment
Of Christ-in-us distinct and yet the same,
Who makes, and loves, and keeps us in each moment,
And looks on us with pity not with blame.
Keep telling me, for all my faith may waver,
Love is his meaning, only love, for ever.

65

Death Be Not Proud

April has indeed become the cruellest month. Even as life blossoms in our gardens, death stalks our streets and hospitals. As Henry Scott Holland lamented a century ago, in the passage from his sermon that nobody quotes:

> 'But how often death smites, without discrimination, as if it had no law! It makes its horrible breach in our gladness with careless and inhuman disregard of us.'

And now we must fight on through grief, resisting an enemy that seems to have defeated our friends while the indifferent April sun shines on. And shall we keep Easter in spite of the grief, in spite of churches locked and empty, in spite of packed hospitals, exhausted doctors and nurses, clergy and carers pushed past their limits?

Yes, we shall keep Easter, and not in spite of these things but because of them. For it was into the cruellest of Aprils that Christ came to find and save us. He came to take on death at its worst; to experience for us, with us and in us that hideous combination of exposure and isolation that was his cross; to know with us what it feels like to perish within and yet beyond the reach of the ones we love.

But if he shares our Good Friday, and especially this dark one we are all sharing now, it is so that we can share his Easter. On this strange Easter Sunday we will discover that he is not lost somewhere in our locked churches, any more than he was sealed in the sepulchre. He is up and out and risen long before us. He is as much at work in the world as the spring is at work in the blossoms. On this Easter Sunday the Risen Christ, who might have been a wafer in the hands of the priest, will be strength in the hands of the nurse, a blessing in the hands of the carer. He goes with them to their work as surely as he came to us in our church.

Victory over this virus is some way off but victory over death is already achieved. It was because he knew that in Christ 'death is swallowed up in victory' that Henry Scott Holland was finally able to say 'Death is nothing at all'.

A Dean of St Pauls who lived through just such times as ours had said that before, with even greater power. John Donne saw more than his fair share of 'poison, war, and sickness' but he could still fling this great defiance into the face of death. It is Christ's defiance and, this Easter, it is ours:

Death, be not proud, though some have called thee
Mighty and dreadful, for thou art not so;
For those whom thou think'st thou dost overthrow
Die not, poor Death, nor yet canst thou kill me.
From rest and sleep, which but thy pictures be,
Much pleasure; then from thee much more must flow,
And soonest our best men with thee do go,
Rest of their bones, and soul's delivery.
Thou art slave to fate, chance, kings, and desperate men,
And dost with poison, war, and sickness dwell,
And poppy or charms can make us sleep as well
And better than thy stroke; why swell'st thou then?
One short sleep past, we wake eternally
And death shall be no more; Death, thou shalt die.